CW00552051

Published by Zebra Press
(a division of the New Holland Struik Publishing Group (Pty) Ltd)
PO Box 5563, Rivonia, 2128
Tel: 27 11 807 2292
Fax: 27 11 803 1783

Published work © Zebra Press 2000

Managing editor Marika Truter
Designed by Braam Kruger
Typeset by Amanda van Rhyn & Denise Meredith
Text © Braam Kruger
Artworks © Braam Kruger
Photography © Braam Kruger

These recipes & articles have appeared in *Business Day*.

Printed and bound by Trident Press (Pty) Ltd, Cape Town

ISBN 1 86872 249 X

CONTENTS

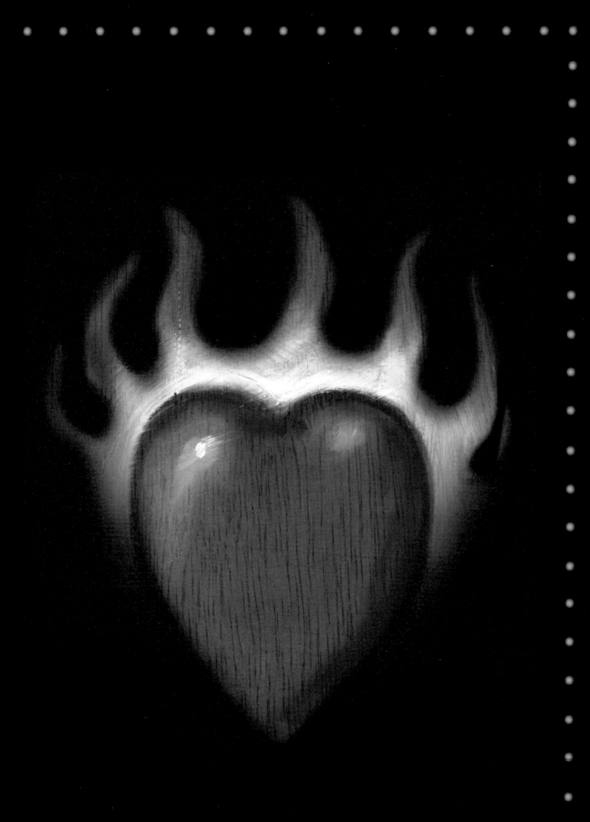

Kitchenboy IN LOVE

Kitchenboy believes the meaning of art is entirely up to the viewer. In this reworked drawing of his, he simultaneously saw how his new love saved him from certain hedonistic destruction and how incredibly vulnerable it left him emotionally.

~~JUNGLE FEVER~~

KITCHENBOY IN LOVE

Your wildly callous and philandering old bliksem **Kitchenboy**, who peddles with flirting words, pictures & provocative notions on food, art and sexuality to earn a dubious living, capitulated head first into love. He lost his flaming heart to the youthful Junglegirl under a full moon on a tropical beach, which left him speechless, humbled and in awe and wonderment of her glorious being.

How infinitely desirable is that exhilaratingly beautiful condition when two people are covered in invisible electric sparklers, wandering about in slow motion with an eerie reborn light emanating from beyond their eyes, while time stands still around their new awareness, heightened creativity and intense generosity and care for each other? And they rediscover & reinvent themselves to share and reshape their vulnerable values, symbols, fantasies, secrets, desires, doubts and dreams. Surely this must be the opposite extremity of all darkness.

During one rare flash of reality, I realised how terrifyingly unequipped I would be should this chemical euphoria be whipped out of my bloodstream for whatever reason. How utterly unprepared I am to take a fall back to whence I came. How we set ourselves up for disappointment with hopes & dreams of the future. And how we have only ourselves to blame for believing so often in something which wasn't there in the first place.

Memories of former ecstasies in a relationship may be bathed in honey & romance, but this remains a highly personalised interpretation and certainly doesn't belong to the realm of the real any more. So too are our unrealistic expectations of what is to come, those forever-ever fables which run care-free & oblivious to the perils of the real world like a simple but devastating switch of heart or loyalty, a slip down the staircase, crime, mortality and catastrophes.

But this very specific little moment, this expansive and enriching experience you are sharing with someone in the here and the now, is all there really is, the only tangible time frame which represents your compassion for each other. Food in itself has little spiritual nourishment compared to food shared with love, without which it is stripped bare of all meaning.

It was an awesomely inspired long-distance courtship, that which moulded the fable of Kitchenboy & Junglegirl. A month after he had left St Lucia with a hole in his heart, he finally & anxiously fetched her from the airport, to embrace their new life together. On their virgin night in her new home, in his loving quest to please her, and thank her, oh thank you so very much, for making that moment, and all those to follow, a fairy tale, he prepared this deceptively modest little dish for her approval. It also represented the new cuisine she was letting herself in for, so foreign to her sweet & silky palate, and in many ways, my best shot. Moreover, the Japanese believe that every new food to pass your lips for the first time prolongs your life by 75 days.

I had met ace New Zealand chef Rick Rutledge-Manning a few months before Junglegirl's arrival, while I was hosting the Cape Gourmet Festival. He kindly gave me the recipe for this sublime and elegant starter.

KB & Junglegirl on the Mzenen River, Phinda Game Reserve, before she finally migrated to Johannesburg.

JUNGLE FEVER

SEARED TUNA WITH PEPPER-DHANIA CRUST
ON A SALAD WITH CHINESE ROCK SUGAR DRESSING

DRESSING
50 g Chinese rock sugar, crushed
50 ml rice vinegar
50 ml white vinegar
50 ml rice wine (mirin)
10 ml soy sauce (Kikkoman)
15 g fresh ginger, chopped
1 small onion, sliced
2 cloves garlic, crushed
1 spring onion, chopped
15 ml dhania, chopped

• Melt the rock sugar in a mixture of both types of vinegar.
• Add rice wine (mirin) & soy sauce. • Add to aromatics & infuse for 3 hours.

SEARED TUNA
300 g super-fresh tuna, cut into a 5 cm cylinder
2 tbsp roughly cracked black pepper
4 tbsp basil, finely chopped
1 tbsp dhania, finely chopped
salt
60 ml olive oil

• Mix pepper & herbs & roll tuna therein to cover well. • Wrap tightly in cling wrap to keep shape till ready to cook. • Season with salt & sear quickly in a little olive oil. Don't overdo or outside will flake. Aim for the thinnest possible whitening of crust, remaining raw inside. • Allow to cool.

SALAD
400 g cucumber, cored & cut into short sticks
120 g snow peas, blanched
a handful bean sprouts
wasabi

TO ASSEMBLE
• Build a small salad stack in the centre of the plate. • Drizzle a little dressing over the salad and a bit more to puddle in the plate. • Slice tuna into 1 cm-thick discs and stack 3 or 4 around the salad. • Garnish with dhania sprig & dot the edge with *wasabi*.

Serve with affection and tell your partner you love him or her, don't just think it, and you will capture that fleeting delicate moment forever.
For food, indeed, can and should be pure love.

Typical Kitchenboy Art (KitchArt), camping up the Old Masters. *Venus or Eve's Tree of Life* is loaded with tits, naturally, the foliage covering the only fig in the picture.

APHRODISIACS

A table-to-pillow guide for the New Millennium, for New Age persoontjies, as rated & whispered by your resident hedonist Kitchenboy. He can talk about food & sex for hours on end, and often does, but always runs out of space and time. Put on your robe, pour yourself a dry martini and make yourself comfortable. Hands on the table.

One late night after a party, I was led home by a cheeky & handsome gay girl, on condition, naturally, that I behave. Which I did a little. But then she transformed into one of the sweetest, most caring and passionate lovers I have ever been with. The woman-man thing never even featured. Together we discovered the magic of gentle massaging with good quality extra-virgin olive oil, the only slithery stuff we could find, to wake up at high noon, with radiating satin skins covering our persons. And we were beautiful. And the world was beautiful, as we languidly lunched on wild oysters and *sashimi*, which had all the enchantment & persuasiveness it would have had the night before. It was only a deadline which forced me back to my damn desk. The subject was by now a foregone conclusion.

To write about food, I have to be hungry. I mean really hungry, which is the feeding ground of all deliciousness. But to write about food and seduction, I figured, wasn't about being all ramkat & horny: I simply had to feel good about myself. And about others. As I do today. So this is not a vulgar old-timer's gender guide, manne conquering girls & all that. It is about recognising the other individual as one with the same imagination, wickedness, needs & sexuality as yourself. To be respected for who they are and, the most important aphrodisiac of all, to be ADORED.

OYSTERS *****
No argument about their powers. But you will be shocked to know how many people avoid them. What a score if you could feed

SASHIMI *****

True *sashimi*-grade raw fish, with hardly a whisper of the ocean, exquisitely presented by a master, is my sexiest food in all the world. A little dab of *wasabi*, a trickle-dip in the very best soy sauce, followed by a sliver of *gari* (pickled ginger) and hair-cut daikon radish to prepare your mouth for the next entry.

caviar, which comes from one of the sturgeon species from the Caspian Sea (beached by Russia or Iran). Large berries from the beluga sturgeon, smaller from the ostra & smallest from the sevruga. Avoid pasteurised caviar. But again, find a reliable (no, passionate) supplier. Lumpfish eggs don't qualify, ou Maat, and those translucent salmon or trout thingies are fun enough,

APHRODISIACS

when you manage to align them with a row of teeth to pop, or to find them in another's mouth during the night. No toast please, not everybody visits you with a toothbrush in their pocket and anyway, they interfere with the mysteriously evasive, creamy flavour of true caviar. A morsel of a blini underneath perhaps, but best of all, fed by you with a mother-of-pearl spoon or oyster shell. Or think of something even better. I can.

SUSHI *

It boggles my mind that it is considered sex food. Pretty and alluring, yes. But rice clogs one's teeth and the Japanese government runs annual campaigns, warning against choking on compressed rice cakes. Asphyxia is hardly a foreplay activity. Ask Bubbles Schroeder.

ASPARAGUS *

What wanking nonsense that this is an aphrodisiac! One of those oke-extensions again, like walking around with a gun. This phallic shoot from the lily family (like onion & leek) excretes seriously smelly methyl mercaptan into your urine. Previously thought to affect only prone individuals, so-called 'stinkers'. It is now certain that it affects everybody likewise, but only some can detect it. That might be your partner.

EXTRA-VIRGIN OLIVE OIL *****

You better believe it.

CONSIDERATIONS *****

As an artist & caring host, your lascivious Kitchenboy has a whole rail of kimonos & robes to choose from, before & after posing, swimming, sauna, shower, bubblebath or anything wet, actually. It turns everyone into relaxed and darling beings, even if they just sleep over, as many friendgirls under his devious protection often do. We are all shy at heart and in the waiting nether regions. And consideration is by far the most darling part of seduction.

That's why he has new toothbrushes and a beautiful vase of tampons & condoms in his bathroom. Always had.

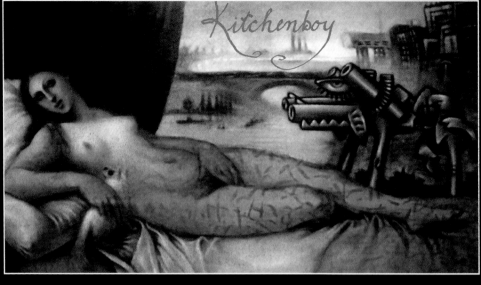

Venus with Metal Dog, (oil on wood panel), is KB's favourite nude painting and the genre dearest to him. In a wicked way, he feels he thus gives the classical artists options they never had in their generation.

DINING, DRUGS & TABLE MANNERS

A notorious old boozer, party animal and professional hedonist, your rampant Kitchenboy can hardly be described as a prude or moral koek. But substance abuse & related issues have become so common in contemporary society that they can no longer be naïvely shoved under the tablecloth by thoughtful hosts & guests alike. Gooi 'n dop, relax, and share with him some observations & ramblings on the impact this has on dinner parties, entertaining and sex.

I stupidly started smoking again after fifteen years, initially to complement, or rather bear, kissing a smoking partner – which is not unlike licking out a dirty ashtray. Apart from giving new meaning to chain smoking, it also highlighted for me the barbarity of this absurd & fatal habit. Having that ever-present skyf and cigarette ash is not only unsavoury cooking practice, but the fouling of your taste buds affects your ability to make continual nuance adjustments to the flavouring of dishes, the very essence of serious cooking. Even as a non-smoker, however, I never proscribed smoking at my table after each course, and if you are going to be such a toegeknypte host, you should say so by invitation. I won't come.

Cigars are so fashionable now that they are unavoidable, but there is much to be said for the civilised smoking rooms & lounges of bygone eras. I must have fallen for all the hype, for a woman with a cigar in her mouth is so sexy that I can faint, all for the wrong reasons, of course. I hate myself, I hate myself, okay? Strictly a both-activity. Ditto smoking in the bedroom, but I guess that also depends on who you're with & the nature of your indulgence. Personally, I've never seen

DINING, DRUGS &
TABLE MANNERS

anything endearing come from taboos & guilt in that sanctuary of liberation & discovery.

I love being drunk, no escaping that, and so do most of my friends; but arriving plastered for a dinner date is utterly unforgivable – I'd rather you stood me up. Either way, you're off my invitation list. Being the officially sanctioned drug by both government (for its tax revenue) and society (for its legality), I secretly judge the success of a dinner party by counting the wine bottles in the morning and the bodies littering my mansion. The criminality and dangers of drunken driving oblige you as a caring and/or seducing host to plan a feast with this well in mind. Provide optional sleeping arrangements for your guests, as well as new toothbrushes, basic cosmetics, fresh towels, headache pills, hangover cures and a fortifying breakfast to repair the damage you've caused, albeit willingly.

If you are cooking with alcohol and have a guest who is trying to control a drinking problem, or abstains for religious or other reasons, burn off the alcohol early in the process with the lid off. It has a much lower evaporation temperature than water. But never ever use it neat in trifles & other cold fare. Inform them discreetly about the contents of the dish. You don't want to wreck someone's life; you want to add to the magnificence of it.

I have known many charming people who find it stimulating and calming to hit a joint before social and erotic encounters, even if dope simply transforms me into a hapless bride with a spinning headache. But I deeply resent the nauseating smell of dagga where I am presenting carefully composed aromas & flavours, to speak not of those concentrated gagga breaths of dope-heads, and worse, the impairment of their lustreless

DINING, DRUGS & TABLE MANNERS

intellectual contribution and appreciation of lovingly prepared food. So old China, you wannabe cool, then strictly after dinner and only outside, not to implicate your host in the illegal substance on their property.

Cooking with dope is not without interest to the culinary curious. I even have a whole book on the subject by a committed old hippy, but he too concedes that such experiments are flawed by the question of dosage. Not everyone has the same tolerance level. On a few occasions I have been fed it unwittingly in seemingly innocent dishes, with near catastrophic implications for my date & me. It is not funny, nor hip or daring. It is cruel, criminal and lavishly uncool in a consenting society. The same goes for drugging the cocktail or punch of a date, jou bliksem.

Cocaine instantly takes away your appetite, and I had to watch

many a dedicated dish stand untouched till dawn by pre-dinner snorters. It is the rudest act of disrespect to a host I can think of. It might keep you awake till dawn, but men invariably end up embarrassed about their hardcore performance, and leaving their highly aroused partner frustrated at their lack thereof. And as they say, speed kills.

Kitchenboy has much empathy with eating disorders, their social causes and self-destructive effects. They merit all your care and understanding. On vomiting *per se* he has a simple view. Food should make you feel good and nourished. If your system tells you it doesn't, just go & do it. Guilt is pointless self-flagellation. Who wants to go to bed with someone who feels awful and might get sick there anyway? If it's not you, have another drink, turn up the music & let them handle it. They'll soon recover. Actually, they always do.

Painted from a ham KB made himself, this painting has strong sensual overtones. He never understood the sexual symbolism of figs before he had a Mediterranean lover.

Youthful actress Nicole Abel (aka Vodagirl), was to become KB's best friendgirl, at a bonfire during a bizarre game festival in his hometown, Nigel.

From time immemorial diners would become restless & peckish before the arrival of the main course, getting your uptight Kitchenboy into a toestand, while he should be concentrating on the last important touches to his creations. That's why he invented the starter (vrooom-vrooom), the *hors d'œuvre* (literally: outside the work) and the antipasto (before meal), that frivolous bit of playfood to amuse and placate your guests during the final countdown.

These little teasers have become so fashionably elaborate in the hands of ambitious chefs that we have forgotten the purpose of it all: to keep diners occupied. One of the earliest recorded starters was simply fresh figs wrapped in ham. Nothing wrong with that, especially if you land some fresh black figs with their gorgeously erotic scarlet flesh, and pair them with paper-thin slivers of uncooked air-cured ham like Parma, which is more commonly married to green winter melon or spanspek. I will invariably choose this over any restaurant's peacock creation. The incredibly perfumed orange variety of melon (cantaloupe) wasn't always known as spanspek in SA but as meloen, when it was among the first fruits harvested from the Company Gardens at the Cape. One of the last governors had a Spanish wife who would have no bacon (spek) at breakfast, but only melon. And so it became teasingly known as Spaansche spek among the kitchen staff of the Fort.

To pick the best spanspek from the stack, sniff at the navel for the most fragrant aroma. Perfectly ripe green melons have a waxy skin and little smell, but give slightly when pressed around the navel. Any fruit & cured meat will do just dandy. Hey, I was raised on naartjies & biltong. Amabokkebokke!!!

DUKKAH

Bread is often overlooked as a starter, but served anyway as sommer-so. The ancient way of enjoying bread – that is before margarine & Marmite – was to dip it into olive oil & then into chopped herbs and/ or nuts. This is what the Persians called Dukkah. It is still the favourite starter at my table. The real success of Dukkah is determined by the uncompromising quality of the ingredients. Tough-textured rustic bread like Italian *ciabatta* (literally slipper), chewy Portuguese *bolo do caco* (stone cake, which uses sweet potato), freshly baked Greek *pita* (from classical Greek *peptos* meaning 'cooked') or napkin-soft Indian tandoori baked naan. See, compared to stuff like that, bread rolls or government loaves simply won't do.

Slowmow (aka Lloyd Ross), KB's dear friend &
patient TV director

DUKKAH

Use only the best extra-virgin olive oil you can afford and try to include as many of the listed fresh herbs you can find.

A handful of each or any of the following:
mint
parsley
basil
rosemary
dhania (aka fresh coriander)
rocket
thyme
sage
origanum
chervil

- Remove all woody stems & chop fairly coarsely by hand (or pulse briefly in processor, but do not mince).
- To serve, put out two bowls or bakkies where all diners can reach them: one containing chopped herbs, the other olive oil.
- Heat the whole bread in foil in an oven, or wrapped in paper or a napkin in a microwave (maximum 30 seconds).
- Wrap in a large napkin to keep warm.
- Demonstrate to your baffled guests how to go about it: tear off a piece of bread & dip it first into the oil, then smear/press it into the herbs till they stick to the wet spot. Bite off just short of your fingertips. Take a sip of wine and leave your guests to indulge while you sneak back to the kitchen.

Hysterically amused by the presumed difference between good & bad taste, in art as in food, this picture was a marvellous opportunity to combine them. The painting was commissioned by a patron with an avocado-crocodile farm.

Kiekie, Fairy & Junglegirl, in the limousine she hired for KB's surprise 50th birthday party.

~~AVOCADO~~

NEW WAVE AVO RITZ

'SUPERTRASH!!!' yells the dark side of your rubbishy Kitchenboy, as he gallops through the valleys and mists of time, to where a classical Venus awakens to the steaming New World, beside an *ahuacatl*. Translated from the Aztec as 'testicle tree', it was bashfully corrupted by Venus to avocado (aka avocado pear and, formerly, alligator pear).

From time to time, pressure is brought upon me by my friends to concede that popular peasant food, of the non-gourmet variety, isn't really so bad after all. Truth is, when you're forever designing, testing and cooking supercilious food, the compulsion to dive into street-level gastronomy is urgent to the point of becoming a secret perversion. You have no idea how many top chefs I know binge on sardines & toast. Few dishes epitomise this lowliness as well as the South African-born Avocado Ritz from the 60s, cloned from the tacky Prawn Cocktail of the British. Oho, excuse me, sir, avo is a damn sight better than shredded iceberg lettuce. And since retro food is determined to be the latest trend, I shall presently introduce you to the camp Kitchenboy Avo Ritz, a radiantly farcical starter for your next pool party. Actually, at the risk of rubbing your nose in it, I originally redesigned this dish for a hoaxy Bad Taste Menu in a magazine.

Make no mistake about it, the cold marriage of crustacean, avocado and a piquant mayonnaise harmonises beautifully, even if it is so surreptitiously avoided in the East, as is avo altogether. And no, a California *Sushi* Roll is real live American junk. To my grief, crab & kreef are also often used in these 'seafood cocktails'. Vommie!

It was in the hands of the gorillas of the café kitchens where it all went wrong, starting with those tiny, maggoty, tasteless, pre-cooked shrimps, churned up with a heinous Thousand Island Dressing of mayo and tomato sauce, as we call it. To my shame, I have to confess: The Fairy (my chief gastronomist) and I tried diligently to elevate the Thousand Island Dressing to a higher level, but finally gave in. The dish actually needs a wishy-washy trashiness. So we tested all prevailing commercial Thousand Island Dressings, to settle on the best of the worst. But what to do with those ubiquitous sprigs of parsley, which I have never seen anybody sober eat? So I chopped them fine and planted them as a colonial lawn atop the avo island as part of a secret joke about shark-infested mayo.

Flash (aka Nicholas Gordon), dedicated ex-PA & friend who taught KB telephone man-ners & computer stunts.

Tarzan, eldest son of KB, with wrist-guard after a slip into the swimming pool, which left him very wary of water.

AVOCADO

NEW WAVE AVOCADO RITZ

16 large whole prawns
1 handful coarse salt
butter, for grilling
2 cloves garlic, bruised
2 large & firm avocados
1 small bunch parsley, finely chopped
1 bottle Thousand Island Dressing (Steers)
2 large fresh red chillies, sliced
cocktail dekorasies

- Devein prawns with a toothpick, sprinkle salt over
and leave for 20 minutes.
- Then rinse & dry. Skewer temporarily to keep straight.
- Fry in butter with the garlic, about 1 minute a side,
till barely cooked.
- Slice the avos in half (to remove the stone from the other half,
whack a sharp knife into the stone and twist out).
(Not in your palm, please).
- Carefully peel and roll the outsides in the parsley to coat.
- Place open concave side down on a plate.
- Pour dressing thickly over rest of plate and draw
waves into it with your clean finger.
- Sprinkle chilli flotsam on edge of waves.
- Dock prawns whole or shelled beside the avo, which you
decorate with umbrella, flags or other cocktail sillies.

The island cartoon, which evolved from teenage drawing to KB's symbol of his time and personal immortality.

A fairly innocent play-tattoo of a dragon initiated the fable of Kitchenboy & Junglegirl.

COCONUT MILK & MUSSEL SOUP

That surrealistically silly cartoon has been around for as long as your beach-combing Kitchenboy cares to remember. You know, the desolate island thing, decorated with a coconut palm, complete with circling sharks and scantily clad poppie who never grows a day older. It has also become the symbol of his time and generation, a tattoo of his romantic fascination with tropical island cuisine.

A most grateful tree it is, cruising ocean currents till it washes up against a shore and plants itself at the spring-tide mark, bearing 70 to 120 coconuts a year until it eventually dies of old age at around 80 to 100 years. Just like a native man, like me. My wish is to have my ashes planted under a young palm, so that my spirit can be drawn up into it, and so attain immortality. Apart from its enterprising usefulness as material for cloth & carpets, boats & sails, ropes, lamps & oil, roofing, timber and fuel, it is remarkably versatile as food. Feeding its peasant owner for a lifetime.

The bud at the top, aptly called heart of palm, is a vulgar delicacy. Harvesting it kills the tree (shame man), the very reason your sentimental Kitchenboy vowed never to partake in that sacred flesh. But the palm generously yields an amber sap from which sugar is boiled and poured into half-coconut moulds. Its peculiar sweetness has no equal in subtlety. This sap also ferments naturally into a heady wine, which turns into the most delicate vinegar I have ever encountered.

To choose a coconut, shake and listen to the liquid inside, the more slosh the fresher the nut. But please, this is the refreshing & ever so drinkable coconut juice, and NOT coconut milk, as I often overhear. That is a bit more difficult to come by. You have 3 options, and sensing your allergy to exasperating gastronomical excercise, please find them listed in order of laziness. 1. Buy a can. That's it, damn easy and almost faultless (with a tiny zing from being canned, but not everyone knows as much as I do). 2. Or whirrrrrr together equal volumes of dried desiccated coconut and boiling water in a processor for about a minute, let it cool (or burn your fingers), dump it into a (clean) cloth and squeeze the liquid into a bowl. Voila! Coconut milk. 3. Or you can manufacture it likewise with freshly grated coconut flesh, prised from the cracked open nut, but I get tired just thinking of making it, even if it is the best of all.

Kitchenboy has often wondered if the Asians' curious lactic intolerance (after weaning, they lose their ability to digest milk) is the reason for their invention & love of coconut milk, particularly in tropical South East Asia. To partake in the magic of this marvellous and nourishing ingredient, clamber onto the rocks and collect your quota of black mussels, and concoct this intoxicating recipe.

Welsh chef Graham Jones & manager Riecz Ganzewietz, during a rare break at the infamous but brilliant Kitchenboy Restaurant, rendezvous of the international media, 1995

COCONUT PALMS

COCONUT MILK & MUSSEL SOUP

1 can coconut milk (or home-made)

1 can water

½ cup lemon juice

3 tbsp *nam pla* (Thai fish sauce) (or light soy sauce)

2 tbsp palm sugar (or golden brown sugar)

zest of 1 lemon (or lemon grass or a few citrus leaves)

1 tbsp fresh ginger, shredded

1 tsp garlic, chopped

1 cup dhania, chopped

a handful fresh mussels

1 tsp per serving bowl of chilli paste

- Heat all except last three ingredients till the sugar dissolves.
- **DO NOT BOIL** (it will curdle).
- Add dhania & mussels near boiling point and cook timidly until mussels open or heat through.
- Dollop the chilli paste in each bowl and ladle in some soup & mussels.
- Garnish with lemon peel & dhania sprigs.

Dearest friendgirl & dedicated actor, Cat Andrew, in the
KB dining room

Nude of ex-girlfriend Isabella Smook, to whom the commercial salad dressing was dedicated. The idea was to create several dressings, named after special women in the life of KB.

Lee & Robert Brozin, CEO of Nando's, friend, unflinching patron and business associate of KB from the outset.

GIRLFRIEND SALAD

Composing a salad is like making love. And nobody understands this better than your incurably romantic Kitchenboy, who has experienced more magic with women than he could ever narrate on this inhibited page. And who has seduced more beautiful people with wicked food than he can possibly remember.

The following comes from an old letter, stuck on a jar, (to the nude in my picture):

'Isabella, my gorgeous Angel,

What precious memories I have of our times together.
And of your romantic salads & daring dressings,
mystical creations to entice your curious greeneries past my lips, my mouth. How well I remember your half-closed eyes,
your mesmerising lashes blinking in slow motion against my face.
Oh, violate me again like that, and again and again,
so orally and profoundly unforgettable.

And so I shall spread the legend, my Love,
of Kitchenboy & Isabella,
and the extraordinary salad dressing that was born from our rare liaison.

Because there is nothing I desire more than pleasing you.
Your Kitchenboy forever.'

To make a Girlfriend Salad requires the daintiest of touches; nothing about it may seem cluttered or forced, which is why you need a very large flat platter or even a tray. I always raise my hands above my head and let the leaves, herbs and flowers flutter down casually, making sure much of the plate is still visible. My reasoning being that chance has more elegance than any *ikebana* master.

Use whatever leaves & herbs are available, but two very definite no-nos are the café-ish iceberg and butter lettuces. Two minutes of contact with vinegar and they look as if a lorry drove over them.

leaves. Even better if you enhance it with some pretty bitter/smoky leaves like radicchio, *witloof* (aka chicory), endive, rocket, etc. Then some fresh herbs like torn basil, dhania, dill, etc. And edible flowers, you old charmer, you, like roses, violets, carnations and nasturtiums. Because the Girlfriend Dressing is OIL FREE, unlike other dressings, we can cheerfully add fruit to our salad. This is going to bring great colour and excitement to your platter. Carefully place creatively cut fruit among the leaves on the edge

naartjie segments, fan-cut apple or pear, banana halved lengthways, strawberries, etc. etc. etc. Don't let me hold you back.

The heart of the salad is going to transform it into a fully balanced meal, perfect for a summer lunch by the poolside. Again, because the dressing contains no oil, we can arrange some delicious meat in the centre of the salad. Slivered, cold roast beef fillet, hot grilled chicken breast, barbecued tuna, steamed mussels, clams or crayfish, grilled calamari and so on and so on.

The notorious and cantankerous Kitchmobile (aka KMb) in the Drakensberg, official KB vehicle & star of many TV inserts.

GIRLFRIEND SALAD

GIRLFRIEND DRESSING

100 ml cider vinegar
2 tbsp white sugar
1 tsp fresh ginger, finely chopped
1 tsp garlic, finely chopped
1 tsp red chilli, finely chopped
4 tsp fresh basil (or other herbs), finely chopped
1 tsp lemon zest, finely chopped (use a potato peeler)

Now you simply shake up the dressing and drizzle it lavishly over leaf, fruit and meat. Ultimately, this dressing is the mesmerising factor that marries all the ingredients. Believe me, you now have an addiction on hand. I usually make the dressing up in a recycled nip bottle, then she can take it as a breast flask to restaurants. I have even seen them gargling down the stuff after a heady night.

Grethe Fox, brilliant actor & gorgeous ex-girlfriend, whose fabulous salad dressings initiated the notion of

Kitchenboy

That blerrie island thing again, designed as an award for a frequent Saturday breakfast club organised by KB.

Swim-gear, a gift from ex-girlfriend Lynn Radford; a failed attempt to lure him

BEACHBUM'S
GUIDE

Your seafood-crazy Kitchenboy leads you through the tidal zone in this alternative beachbum's crash course on shellfish cooking. Whether it opens, closes, floats, crawls, slithers, pinches, squirts, stings, bites or sucks, he has probably eaten it. So let him guide you through the simple pleasures and perils of enjoying the noble fruits of the sea, right there on the rocks or on the beach.

Those of you who are sensibly paranoid about the dangers of eating seafood, relax, you are in safe hands. Since freshness is not an issue for beachcombers, the only real danger is RED TIDE, and the only shellfish affected by it are the filter-feeders, and they are invariably bivalves (i.e. double-shelled snaily creatures). Because they are filter-feeders, the residue of toxins and pollutants is incredibly concentrated inside their little persoontjies (an oyster pumps almost 100 litres of seawater in 24 hours).

Even if eating seafood still scares you, that leaves you with most of the other seriously consumable sea creatures, which are herbivorous, predators and scavengers. But for your peace of mind, I shall start cautiously with the delicate, albeit precarious, bivalves. After that it is carefree surfing.

BIVALVES
These are all filter-feeders, so get official confirmation (the locals know boggerol) that your stretch of sea is clear of recent or current red tide. Do remember that all shellfish are eminently edible raw, and they are literally only heated to get them out of their shells.

OYSTERS
Once you have been perverted by sensational wild oysters, as I have, you will never tolerate those watery cultivated things again. Shucking them is an art, so take care with that knife. Open with the flat-roof shell uppermost so the seawater

~~BEACHBUM'S~~ ~~GUIDE~~

remains in the hollow bottom: it is the only flavouring needed. This mother of the sea and the pearl (hence perle+moer) *must* be savoured raw, no matter what you've read. Swig it from the shell, at a push with a dash of Tabasco or pepper & lemon juice. Or drop one into a glass of quality bubbly for a Kitchenboy oyster shooter. And for God's sake, don't swallow it whole: chew it till your eyes start rolling in your head.

BLACK MUSSEL

(Female's flesh chocolate brown, males are pale yellow.) Heat only until open, please, please, please, just enough to set the plump flesh. Any longer and the meat shrinks and dries dramatically. A simple & delicious way to cook mussels is standing them shell-down on the hot edge of a stone at your campfire till they open. Or think of pop-

corn. Use a lekker big pot (they expand when opening) with a tight-fitting lid (to keep the steam circulating). Heat on a fast fire, with or without a splash of liquid (seawater, wine, beer, cider or their own leaking moisture). Shake pot continually and peek after 2 to 3 minutes for openness. Alternatively, clamp between layers of seaweed on grill over low coals.

BROWN MUSSEL

Ditto (females bright orange, males off-white).

MEDITERRANEAN MUSSEL

Ditto (females orange, males off-white).

WHITE MUSSEL

(Aka wedge shell.) Jived out on wave-exposed beaches, mostly for bait. Hugely underrated, sweet flesh. Prepare as for mussels.

BEACHBUM'S GUIDE

PENCIL BAIT

(aka razor clam). Barely heat in a splash of water or booze (with a knob of butter), sublime – sadly used as bait.

CLAMS

Very sandy, so stand in a bucket of seawater to expel sand grains. Lightly steam or boil in seawater or soup.

GASTROPODS

Being herbivorous, predators & scavengers, these are entirely safe from red tides and the like. Again, to be heated through only, exactly when they can be extracted from the shell.

WINKLES

(aka periwinkles & topshells). Herbivorous. The various small snails so numerous in the upper tidal zone. I like the larger smooth black one (pink-lipped topshell).

Barely heat through in a little pepper-water till you can extract it with a needle or toothpick. Slide off its plastic trapdoor (operculum) and pop into your mouth with or without a vinegary dressing, dip or butter. Go right ahead, you will *never* get full.

WHELKS

Ditto. Predators & scavengers.

LIMPETS

Herbivorous. Edible (as per above), but hardly rated. I don't like them.

PLOUGHSHELLS

Scavengers, especially on bluebottles & jellyfish. Big foot on a small conical shell, abundant on sandy beaches as the water recedes. Barely heat, extract, pinch off the sandy siphon and munch or reheat in garlic-chilli butter and a squirt of lemon.

Kitchenboy

A painting originally made when Food Editor for *De Kat*. To achieve tender results in cooking molluscs is grossly misunderstood universally. And the island thing again with an ex-girlfriend, sigh...

BEACHBUM'S GUIDE

ALIKREUKEL

(aka turban shell. giant periwinkle). Herbivorous. This large sea snail hides behind an ivory operculum when it withdraws into its shell. and only heat or a hammer is going to get it out of there. Choose the first option and steam or boil in plain water (just over 5 minutes). till trapdoor-lid comes off and the whole shebang can be shaken out. Pinch off the dark poepstring. and devour. dipped in butter garlic sauce or prepare as previous.

ABALONE

(aka perlemoen). Your only chance to enjoy it because nobody can afford it anymore. leading to scary criminal syndicates dealing in abalone. Arguably the most violated food in this country. with most cooks beating. scrubbing and pressure-cooking to get it tender. Listen to me. None of that is necessary. Go Japanese and pack your quota of shells down in a tightly lidded pot. pour some *sake* or other booziness over them and steam till they come out of the shell (usually around 20 minutes). *Not*

a second longer. Slice thinly and dip into good soy sauce. *wasabi* and if it is low tide. tear off the crisp black dried sea lettuce (*Ulva spp*) from the rocks as nori-like accompaniment. and remind yourself how incredibly special that moment is. True beachbums steam them for as long (read short) in the bulb of a sea bamboo. sealed with a stone.

VENUS EAR

(aka siffie). Mermaid-ear-sized abalone. prepared the same way.

CEPHALOPODS

CALAMARI (chokka) and CUTTLEFISH. You're not going to capture any but all bait shops stock them. Boil unsalted water. remove pot from fire. and chuck the calamari in all at once. Twirl around with a stick till water turns milky and flesh turns white and tender. 20 to 59 seconds. and that wasn't a misprint.

OCTOPUS

Another gogga which most people try to demolish before cooking it. by slapping it stupid on the rocks. beating and scouring it till sucker- &

skinless & white (most of the flavour is in said skin). Like per- lemoen, it is totally unnecessary, ineffectual even. Here's a good trick to capture it. With your hand inside a plastic shopping bag, grab it by the head and swiftly pull the open end of the bag over it & make a knot to lock it inside. Put it down and take a stroll. When you return it should be very dead. Turn the head inside out and clean. Hook the head bag on your finger and lower it slowly into plenty of fast-boiling unsalted water. Count to three, slowly, take out and let it cool a little, repeat 3 times. Then drop it into the barely simmering water and leave till tender, sort of. Cool in its cooking water and cut into bits, suckers and all, and warm through in a pan with garlic butter or tomato-onion sauce.

CRUSTACEANS

All crustaceans have a carapace which turns red when cooked, which is when you check one for doneness as the flesh turns from translucent to opaque. Overcooking is the most common sin.

CRAB

Though all crabs are edible, the giant mud crab (wrongly called Knysna crab) is best. Boil in plenty seawater on steam, or wrapped in layers of seaweed, wet newspaper, foil or mud on the coals. Crack shell with stone and dip sweet prized-out meat in melted butter or nibble as is.

Junglegirl on the Mzenen River, Phinda, KB's screensaver.

BEACHBUM'S GUIDE

PRAWNS

You are unlikely to net your own but all those bait prawns the anglers pump are edible. Bait shops also sell them. Who wants to fish? Briefly steam or boil in seawater or beer or cider, pan-fry in garlic butter, but especially brilliant when crisply deep-fried and dipped into a sweet chilli sauce.

ROCK LOBSTER

(aka Kreef and erroneously as spiny lobster or crayfish). Boil in plenty of seawater or steam in water only two fingers deep until bright red. Gooi them uncut on the braai, or halved lengthways on a griddle plate with butter. Whatever you choose, do not overcook; rather leave it a little glassy in the core. And eat as is or dipped in butter & lemon or good soy sauce.

WEIRDOS

SEA URCHIN

Grazers. Cut a teaspoon-sized hole with a scissors on the mouth side (bottom). Peek inside to see the 5 rows of cream- to orange-coloured roe. Carefully shake or rinse out the viscera in the seawater. Spoon out the roe and savour as is or on crackers or toast with a bleep of lemon. Deliciously fruity-sweet.

SEA SQUIRTS

(aka redbait, rooiaas). Many claim to relish this iodine-sodden filter-feeder (take note, prone to red tide poisoning), but as a fisheman who knows it at its worst, it has never attract......attra......ahem.... Vommieeeeee!

The ever-changing menu as KB graffiti on the street-wall of his bygone restaurant.

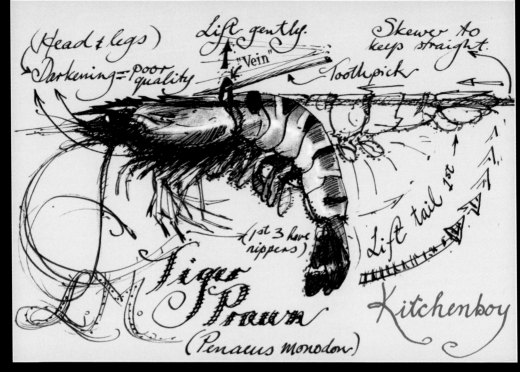

Leonardo Da Vinci's scientific drawings with explanatory notes on deteriorated paper, have a particular fascination for KB, in that they don't pretend to be serious art. Thus his food drawings often pretend to be Leonardo-esque.

A camp KB in his TV costume, tights, pixie-shoes & T-shirt, in the surf of St Lucia during a shoot.

to re-heating, so avoid buying any pre-cooked or blanched prawns, indicated by red-orange shells. This is caused by the hydrocarbon astaxanthin in the carapace, which is actually pink-orange-red but looks grey-blue-black because it is wrapped in a protein, which quickly uncoils during cooking, revealing the actual colour of the astaxanthin molecule. Now you know. Since I have never in my life seen live prawns for sale in SA, I have no problem with neatly packed frozen prawns, but always on the shell. While we're at it, prawns go bad so quickly because of the amino acid glycine, which changes chemically when attacked by bacteria (invariably from poor handling & storage), resulting in that appalling fied by cooking. Because its highly perishable digestive area is housed in the head, blackening of the neck, legs and mouth (called *melanosis* or black spot) is a sure barometer of deterioration. Though harmless and tasteless, it can spread to the meat and this is what I look for when I demand to see the prawns before ordering in a restaurant.

There is, of course, nothing your crafty Kitchenboy can't fix, for he noticed that all Oriental chefs first salt (or even sugar) their prawns for 20 minutes before rinsing & cooking, as they also do with fish. My educated guess is that the sodium neutralises the amino acids, resulting in fresher tasting and firmer prawns. All crustaceans moult (but our disgusting prawns also eat their shells afterwards), which is probably why some individuals are so pap and uncooperative: but why occasional ones should have a tasteless. mealy texture. I have no idea. Snoek does that too.

I know it is a blindly followed tradition to butterfly the prawn from the back and remove the 'vein'. which actually is the poepstring. Sure. this has the advantage of getting the flavour right inside the meat: but without the protection of the shell it also results. more often than not. in utterly overcooked and rubbery prawns – which is a shame at the price. really.

Again. the Orientals devised an ingenious deveining technique (refer to my drawing). Hook the vein with a toothpick at the first or second segment and carefully lift it out. Move down the segments if it breaks. which it shouldn't if you straighten the tail. else it's like pulling a hose around a car tyre. Now you can insert a skewer along the length to prevent the tail from curling. which makes for easier eating & elegant presentations. But most importantly. thus I can cook it aromatically crisp outside. with the flesh still moist. preferably still a little raw in the core. snapping like a cucumber when I bite through the shell. That's the way. aha aha...

KB on his 49th birthday party. giving new meaning to chain-smoking since rediscovering the habit.

PRAWNS

PRAWNS AL DENTE

prawns, any size
lime or lemon juice, fresh
butter
garlic, chopped
blackening spices, masala or piri-piri powder
salt

- Salt, rinse, devein & skewer prawns as explained.
- Squeeze lime or lemon juice directly over them.
- Melt butter and drench over them too.
- Scatter chopped garlic all over.
- Dust with spices of your choice until you get nervous.
Please, never use an open fire, which simply dries them out.
- Sizzle them for a few minutes only over a medium heat on a
metal griddle or some such plate, till they turn
bright orange-red all over.

The Fairy (aka Andrea Bürgener), his beloved
friend, most lateral food companion &
phenomenal chef. When working with KB.

The label for this heartbreak sauce. KB won two Loerie Awards (Silver), for the package designs of the range. He adored the idea of his paintings on supermarket shelves.

~~SEAFOOD~~

THAI GREEN CURRY

You may well wonder why your heartbroken Kitchenboy is sharing a sauce recipe with you which resisted his most zealous efforts to manufacture. But he isn't really lamenting his bad fortune, on the contrary, he's celebrating the fact that some things are just not destined to be commercialised. In the process, he throws a trickle of light on the perils of the sauce-making industry.

It is what I do for a living, which pays the rent, this hectic sauce-manufacturing business (apart from writing, painting and living a life of frantic pandemonium). And I could tell you some pretty hairy stories if you were toying with the idea yourself. The first horror you'll run into is that Consol Glass has a virtual Big Brother monopoly on the glass container industry, a situation that had me weeping on many occasions. Then you'll have to find suitable lids or caps and capping machines, each by different companies, of course. I believe this situation deserves the credit for the recent flood of so-called doy-packs, those hideous filled plastic tubes that feel like limp and sloshing baby beanbags.

Coming up with the concept & recipe for your sauce is by far the least daunting aspect of your enterprise. Your next step would be searching for a willing & reliable manufacturer, and that's another drive-plundering abyss, believe me. And at every stage your product has to be tested by professional laboratories for every gogga and natural reaction invented by God, because your self-respecting Kitchenboy could never consider preservatives or additives, in any case, the contemporary international market won't tolerate them.

To give you some idea, I have

SEAFOOD

been developing and working on eight sauces for almost two years. and spent more on the project than I will personally earn in my lifetime. it seems. The other seven products are fine. my hard-earned pride & joy. to be sure (praise be to God and Jeff Bloch. my patient microbiological friend and consultant). But just this one sauce resisted every attempt at being stuck into a bottle. To add insult to injury. I landed a blerrie Loerie Award (silver) for the label. Nee jong. you have to take your hat off to the Ina Paarmans of this world. for their spirited perseverance.

This marvellous and mild Thai Green Curry. then. belongs to the exclusive domain of the adventurous amateur and restaurant chef. And hey. as the label says. it's groovy with chicken. fish & shellfish. Thai curries are more soupy than the Indian ones. and always start with a paste. as opposed to dry spices. and reap their flavour from both fresh herbs & spices. This amounts to a much fresher & cleaner but still scorching taste. since Thai chillies are justifiably feared the world over.

Claire Johnston. magic vocalist of Mango Groove. caring friend and one of the most beautiful women known to KB.

48

GREEN SEAFOOD CURRY

1 heaped tbsp Thai green curry paste

3 tbsp hot green chilli, chopped

2 tsp garlic, chopped

1 tbsp oil

500 g mixed seafood of your choice

2 cans coconut milk

2 tbsp fresh lime or lemon juice

3 tbsp *nam pla* (Thai fish sauce)

3 tbsp white sugar

5 kaffir lime leaves (or rind of 1 lemon)

1 bunch spring onion tops, finely chopped

1 bunch dhania (aka green coriander), finely chopped

3 tbsp mint or basil, finely chopped

1 handful mixed green vegetables

(i.e. bits of eggplant, cucumber, Chinese greens, French beans etc.)

- Fry the first three ingredients in oil till aromatic.
- Then add the seafood and fry a few seconds longer.
- Add the wet stuff and the sugar, let thicken slightly.
- Add the herbs, stir, then the greens.
- Cut the heat & serve with rice.

Comics were the first encounters KB had with art, and they never lost their charm.

Corner interior of Kitchenboy Restaurant and dazzling young waitron Samantha Babu, who died in a car crash shortly after.

CHOKKA

CHOKKA & CHORIZO

Ag, you know your bashful Kitchenboy isn't one for gushing about his stardom and all that (much). But after a particularly flashy cooking sketch, wherein he revealed his secret to tenderise calamari in but a few seconds, the grateful throngs in the streets grabbed his red-nailed hands, hooting: 'It's true!' Well, (blush), it is.

Chokka is our most abundant species of squid (aka inkfish, calamari & lula to the Portuguese). These peculiar molluscs are plentiful in all the oceans & seas they used to rule (except the Black Sea); and one species, the Jules Vernesque giant squid (*Architeuthis dux*), grows to nearly 20 metres. Eat on that. But you won't find any traditional SA recipes for chokka, damn no, it was classified as bait until some mediocre Italian restaurants taught us in the late 60s to eat it as elastic little crumbed and deep-fried rings. They had us believing calamari actually tastes like that. Well, (now cross), it doesn't.

I accidentally discovered the **Kitchenboy Calamari Trick** ® when I attempted to hasten the defrosting of some frozen squid (jaaaaaa ...)

for a gang of uninvited chommies. I broke the small tubes apart into a large bowl and poured boiling water over them, agitating furiously with a fork to get the heat inside the hoods. Fearing that I might overdo it, I fished one out after a few seconds and instinctively bit through it to see if it ... Oh my God, they're cooked already. So I jaaged to the sink and stopped the process under a running cold-water tap. They were gloriously tender undertooth, and are magical like that in salads and other cold dishes.

But what had me completely nonplussed was that they maintained this tenderness even when further cooked. Indeed, thus blanched & patted dry, they almost instantly coloured when pan-fried.

CHOKKA

deep-fried, grilled, braaied or, spectacularly, wok-fried (check my comic on page 50 under *L Vulgaris* for 'how'd they do that?') The trick's rule of thumb is about 20 seconds for defrosted small mantles, tentacles and rings, to a max of 59 seconds for whole footlong monsters. Missing that, they would need 2 hours to tenderise.

Your ever-scheming Kitchenboy thinks he's got his trickery scientifically cracked, sort of. All cephalopods (squid, octopus & cuttlefish) release a milky fluid upon heating (watch the hot blanching water turn opalescent), which seriously obstructs any efforts to fry, grill or braai them. Wet things don't brown, because water evaporates at 100 °C and that isn't hot enough to caramelise food, right? So the milky fluid keeps coming as you cook and rides between the squid & oil, preventing contact, and by the time it has vaporised, your calamari is tough, truly overcooked and still not browned.

Speaking of culinary tricks, why don't you combine mine with an old piece of Chinese wisdom which will earn you the admiration of all you feed? And it isn't hard to do, really. Here's how. Slit open some medium squid tubes. Holding a scarily sharp knife at a 30 degree angle, with almost no pressure, slice a diamond pattern on the *inside*, but please don't cut right through (see my drawing). Do the boiling water trick and they instantly curl up as the heat shrinks the uncut skin, while the cut side has no surface tension. Not only exquisite to the eye, these little porcupines provide a perfect Pirelli-grip to hold the sauce or dressing of whatever dish you are about to make.

Go try it, and perhaps one day you too will grab my hand in a crowd and whisper: 'It works!' Because it does.

CHOKKA

CHOKKA & CHORIZO

1 handful small calamari hoods
1 handful cooked Chinese wheat or egg noodles
2 tbsp oil for coating noodles
1 loop chorizo sausage
1 red pepper
3 tbsp oil for toss-frying
2 cloves garlic, chopped
1 handful Chinese greens (optional)
1 big blob Chinese black bean sauce (or alternative sauces as below)
Dhania or spring onions, chopped, to garnish

• As with all sussed wok-cooking, prep all the ingredients and have them ready in bowls. • Blanch the defrosted calamari hoods by pouring boiling water over them in a large bowl, agitating continuously till the water turns very milky, from 20 to 30 SECONDS, depending on size. Test one by biting through it. Immediately stop the cooking process under cold running water. Tilt into a colander to dry thoroughly. • Cook the noodles according to type & thickness till al dente. Stop further cooking by draining in a colander or sieve and cool under cold running water (this also removes the glue covering them). Toss lightly in oil to prevent sticking. • Slice the chorizo sausage diagonally (it looks prettier than cut across). • Lop off the two ends of the red pepper, open flat to remove ribs and cut in equal strips • Okay, you are now ready to toss-fry. • Heat the wok over a high gas flame. Pour in the oil in a circle around the edge to lubricate the entire inner surface of the wok, to allow the ingredients to slide freely. • Add the chorizo to toast & release its flavour in the oil. Then the peppers & garlic • Throw in the calamari, closest to the handle, and shake once (hard), to let the 1st ingredients fly and land on top of the calamari. Toast thus, briefly. • Now the noodles, again nearest you, toast till you hear it crackle and toss sharply. • Ditto greens, if using, a few seconds only. • Gooi in the blob or two of black bean sauce, to taste (brands vary in saltiness & heat) or alternative sauce. Toss several times to coat all the ingredients. • Serve immediately & garnish with dhania or spring onion

ALTERNATIVE SAUCES: Gaan mal with your favourite bottled chilli sauce, bean sauce, sweet & sour sauce, chutney, chakalaka and almost anything besides tomato ketchup.

Mother of all Pearls.

Young abalone feeding on kelp

Freshly steamed & sliced

Perlemoen on the rocks

A windblown KB on the Berg River & farmed export cocktail abalone (ie undersized in SA), during a series of TV food sketches on the West Coast

PERLEMOEN

PERLEMOEN ON THE ROCKS

Your self-righteous Kitchenboy works himself up into a toestand when food is utterly misunderstood and then arrogantly mangled in its preparation. That is the consuming fire under his fez for assuming this position as a food writer on a mission to save the world from bad taste.

Abalone (*Haliotis midae*) is hunted as much for its maltreated flesh, or so-called thick 'foot', as its iridescent mother-of-pearl shell. Hence the Afrikaans perlemoen or perlemoer (pearl + mother). Old Cape cookbooks also speak of klipkous and pearl mussel. The equally delicious but much smaller siffie or Venus ear (*H. spadicea*) feeds on red algae, but abalone includes kelp in its diet, making them and you impervious to red tide poisoning. Humanity has practically depleted world stocks of abalone, yet few gourmets treat it with the culinary respect it deserves. In their frustration to render it into the finest seafood God created, they bliksem it to a pulp with rock or mallet, and then proceed to cook it for three or four hours, as even the Japanese sin with their elegant *sake*-steaming. Local seaside per-

lemoen fundis use pressure cookers and then mince & mix the abalone with breadcrumbs into a monster deep-fried frikkadel, served with that ubiquitous white or cheese sauce of boiled-cauliflower fame. What shameful overkill!

For a TV sketch at an abalone farm in Jacobsbaai, on our West Coast, I procured some 'cocktail abalone' and sneaked down to the picturesque little bay, where I steamed them for barely 5 minutes in a lunchbox type fisherman's smoker, seawater replacing the sawdust, of course. You could use any large pot with tight-fitting lid (potjie fine), with a few stones at the bottom to keep them above the boiling seawater. Committed beachbums steam them in the bulb of sea bamboo, sealed with a stone. I noticed that the very beautiful flimsy green sea lettuce (*Ulva spp*) had dried against the rocks in large, crisp black sheets, almost identical to Japanese *nori*, salted by the receding tide. A perfect accompaniment. No kidding. Slices can also be blitz-fried in butter, *half-a-minute a side*, though I find this masks the magic flavour unnecessarily. Although much esteemed raw on *sushi* or as *sashimi* since WWII (blanched before), I find it tough and overrated thus.

KITCHENBOY'S 10-SECOND BLANCHING TRICK

fresh or defrosted frozen perlemoen, out of shell
coarse salt
boiling water

In the sink, sprinkle salt all over perlemoen and let sit for 5 minutes to remove slime and any queer odours. Rinse thoroughly, pat completely dry, and slice like mushrooms, evenly.
Put them in a large bowl and pour lots of boiling water over, agitating with a fork. Start counting ... ...
... not more than 10, till fork or teeth sink in easily.
Immediately stop cooking by refreshing under cold running water. Pat dry and let cool. Decorate with a strip of *nori*, as in *sushi*, arrange beautifully on small plates,
and serve with dipping sauce in next recipe.

Die Cherry op die Koek, a rip-off of an anonymous classic with two prim anties bathing.

PERLEMOEN

PERLEMOEN ON THE ROCKS

fresh perlemoen or siffies in the shell
dried sea lettuce or *nori*
3 parts soy sauce (preferably Kikkoman)
1 part *wasabi*
squeeze of lemon or lime

- Wash the abalone to rid it of sand.
- Put a rack or stones inside a pot or smoker, add 3 fingers of seawater and bring to a fast boil.
- Pack the abalone, shell down, on the rack or stones.
- Slam the lid on tightly & steam for 4 to 8 minutes depending on size. The moment the meat can be levered from the shell with your thumb, it is done.
- Pinch off the dark poepstring, slice thinly like mushrooms and eat with a happie sea lettuce or *nori*, dunked lightly into the soy-*wasabi*-lemon dipping sauce.

Even so, in large specimens, the above method tightens the texture of the surface before the inside is warm. I figured there must a better way to control the crucial timing, so I tried my calamari trick of pouring boiling water over sliced abalone for under 10 SECONDS (described next door), and was delighted with the results. I unconditionally recommend this as the standard of abalone cooking for all time.

The hilarious dish, based on a Chinese deep-frying method, started as a vegetarian joke, evolved out of all recognition and became a flagship steamed dish at the restaurant.

KB with glamorous & accomplished magazine editor, Shona Bagley, who made him Food Editor of Playboy SA, and so initiated the Kitchenboy chain-reaction & became a close friendgirl & regular

CELLOPHANE

CELLOPHANE

SEAFOOD PARCEL

Oh-oh, your haughty Kitchenboy is taking a sideswipe at one of his many culinary aversions: vegetarianism. He sincerely believes he has never met a committed vegetarian foodie; and worse, they all like butternut soup. A sign at the entrance of his bygone restaurant read: *No Unaccompanied Vegetarians Allowed.* But the universe has a way of biting back at you.

Indeed, this dish was born as a tongue-in-cheek send-up of the companions of patrons unfortunate enough to be saddled with a vegetarian for the evening. My heartfelt sympathy found expression in a parcel of highly kitsch, garishly coloured cellophane paper, filled with every conceivable and bizarre fungi from obscure corners of the earth. Topped with some convincing Oriental flavouring, the hysterical parcel was sealed with a metre of opulent plastic-silken ribbon. And finally, as a defiant gastronomical insult, I slammed the whole blerrie thing into a microwave, that heaven-forbidden tool of pretentious cooks. This lantern was then placed on a bed of phonetically complementing puffed cellophane noodles, and the circus on a plate was carried off with playful fanfare to the unsuspecting victim, who was left figuring out how to eat the spectacle with chopsticks.

Hilariously, the joke was on me. It was a stunning invention (ahem), and became one of the benchmark dishes of the restaurant. I have always had a love affair with steaming (which is what microwaving is in this instance) and particularly with parcels, where the flavoured steam is trapped with the food. So I introduced some delectable combinations like mussels & clams with Thai curry, or fish-chicken combos, prawns & tofu (bean curd), calamari & chorizo sausage.

CELLOPHANE

CELLOPHANE

You too can go bananas with your own inventions. Only two rules apply for steaming in a parcel. Any white meat combinations are cool, like shellfish, fish, chicken and even fresh or cured pork. But red meat like lamb, beef and game implodes into yuck under steam; and oily fish like tuna & sardine becomes fishier than fish-fish. The ingredients should all require the same cooking time, by nature or size, so don't put clams and chicken together, unless you have either pre-cooked the chicken or cut it into tiny slivers. This is particularly important when you add vegetables. Cooking times are electrifyingly fast (think of a baby pressure-cooker), particularly for seafood, where a minute or two might do it. Lift parcel and feel underneath, when boiling hot it's done.

Follow my happy snappy-comic clockwise overleaf and hop into your Kitchmobile to get the materials & ingredients. Cut a large square of cellophane & place it over a bowl. Fill it with goodies, no bigger than a fist, flavour and wet them with a little flavoured liquid to give the steam a flying start. Leaving some headspace, tie the neck tightly with the ribbon (to trap the steam). Open out the crown paper to stand proud and microwave. Meanwhile, fluff out the hard bundle of cellophane noodles. With lightning speed, press down with a slotted spoon, deep-fry and remove immediately. They will triple in volume. Drain, place on large platter and nestle the parcel on top.

Tonight, your stoute Kitchenboy will be entertaining a gorgeous woman, who'll have no chicken or red meat past her lips. This is her parcel. She'll never be the same again.

For each parcel:

6 clams
3 baby octopuses, blanched
2 frogs' legs (hee hee)
3 prawns
3 Chinese mushrooms, soaked
clove garlic, chopped
1 chilli, chopped
1 tbsp fresh lime juice (or lemon)
1 tbsp Chinese black bean sauce (or soy or oyster sauce)
oil for deep-frying
1 handful bean thread noodles (aka glass noodles)

A brilliant variation on the lime/black bean sauce is equal measures of palm sugar & rice vinegar, melted.
Use one tbsp to moisten the contents of the parcel.

Angling chum & food writer, Lochner de Kock, camouflaged as an angel for a KB (the artist) TV insert, filmed at a Hindu crematorium. Thus clad, he scared the hell out of the attendant when he walked into the crematorium.

One of the *Black Painting* series, a dark period in his life during his year in Struisbaai, where he fished almost every day and practically lived off the rocks.

HOW TO MANIPULATE YOUR FISHMONGER

A newspaper poster yelled: 36 HANDS LOST AT SEA. Your angling Kitchenboy, champion of the marginalised food producers of our country, felt the pain & shame well up inside him. Is a fish worth a man's life? Pain turned to anger.

Arguably our oldest small industry, generations of fishing communities eke out a desperate living, despite the tempestuous seas, dwindling stocks through over-exploitation, poaching and pollution, crippling restrictions and swamping by giant monopolies. But my deepest resentment is aimed at our hospitality industry, which supports these monopolies for the lazy sake of reliable deliveries, frozen or lame impersonations of what once was a real live thing.

Choose your personal fishmonger suspiciously, interrogate him about his suppliers. Many serious purveyors have connections with small fishing outfits in Mozambique, Sodwana Bay and so forth, which inform the fishmonger of the day's catch that evening, pack his order on ice and send it inland overnight. Some even have their own boats. Sure, it can be pricey, but you are paying tribute to many a brave man's life.

The shocking standard of fishmongering in SA must be blamed squarely on an ignorant, undemanding & apathetic public, and it will only be remedied by your tenacious insistence on quality produce & service. You don't ever have to touch fish before cooking it, providing you tell him *precisely* what you require or aim to do with it, bearing in mind that most I know

BUYING FISH

are poor cooks and shamefully uninformed.

The shop should be scrupulously clean and, like the fish, smell of nothing else than the sea. Fish should be shiny, flesh firm and not leave an indentation when lightly prodded, eyes bright and not pearly or shrunken, and gills bright red. In the absence of gills, open the gill covers and look for bright red cut surfaces, not yet browned by oxidation; or better still, stick your nose in there like fastidious Chinese & Portuguese buyers. Most pre-cut fillets & steaks have a little red muscle down the sides, when this is brown or black the fish is old, finish & klaar.

Whole gutted fish should stand upright like motorcycles in crushed ice, to drain off any liquid. Very few fishmongers know that the dark strip under the membrane along the length of the backbone, the so-called 'clotted blood' of cookbooks, is actually the kidney and contains uric acid, which turns to ammonia (read fishiness) when heated. Insist that they scrape it out. Ask that whole fish be descaled *only*, and inspect it before parcelling, especially around the pectoral fins, for stray scales. The

Antonio Bico, KB's favourite fishmonger, with a fine spotted grunter.

BUYING FISH

horrible practice from the 50s, of snipping off the fins, continues. That makes it impossible to guess where their roots are embedded and dangerous to eat off the bone. Leave the head on, please: a whole fish makes for gorgeous presentation.

Have fillets and steaks cut from whole fish. This makes it easier to judge its freshness, origin of species and gives a fresher cut. Fillets on the skin are far tastier and won't fall apart during cooking, and the same applies to cubes for kebabs, stews & soups. Show with your fingers, as for a dop, how thick you'd like your steaks (minimum of two, like a dop) and point to the cross-section of your choice. The middle cut, behind the ribcage & before the anus is my automatic choice. The skin strapped around it holds it together during cooking and contains only the elementary skeleton. The front section's unsightly loose flap cooks faster than the rest because it is oilier, and harbours many dangerous hidden rib bones.

Therefore, dear Gourmet, before you fry your fish, grill your fishmonger. Both sides. well done.

The Fairy at KB's chalk-menu. She moaned that he never cooked for her alone. So he invited her to a single setting and demonstrated fish in 29 different ways.

Like many of KB's artworks, this painting is done from memory and represents no species in particular, but loosely the seabream family. The can-opener key is not just a visual joke, one can actually peel the skin off most fish, from front to back.

Artist Wimpie Cilliers, KB's gorgeous & devoted ex-wife of 13 years. Few women can challenge her adventurous wardrobe & style. They remain very good friends.

WHOLE FISH

Look at your exasperated Kitchenboy, on his knees in the surf, complete with golden vellies and star-spangled tights. Your homespun harlequin of fine cuisine and most humble servant of the sea. Look at him begging you. Pleeeeze. Give whole fish a chance.

As an artist and fisherman, my most sincere argument for presenting you with a whole fish, would be to consider its beautiful natural form. Aesthetically streamlined, each with its own evolutionary reasons behind its peculiar shape, colour and diet, which affect its habits and ultimately, the texture and flavour on your plate. As a piscatorial cook of some intensity, my belief in the culinary superiority of cooking fish as a whole being, as opposed to a skinless fillet, is unequivocal. But first you have to learn to think like a fish in fire, understand what happens to its flesh when heated. Apart from the queer short muscle bundles of fish, they also have very little connective tissue (collagen), only 3% of their body weight, compared to 15% in mammals. When heated, the insoluble collagen collapses into water-soluble gelatine, the syrupy stuff which gives the flesh an unctuousness one would expect from stewed oxtail. But in fish this gelatine thing happens at a much lower temperature (41 °C) than in meat (60 °C). This explains why cooked fish is so delicate and tends to fall apart when overdone.

THE MAGIC OF GELATINE

Apart from the negligible collagen in your fillet, by far the most of the lip-smacking, flavour-bolstering gelatine of fish comes from the skin and skeleton. And that is also why, excuse me, you don't have a hope in hell of cooking your piteous fillet to the incomparable perfection of Kitchenboy's fish on the bone.

The skin of all scaly fish is eminently edible. Imagine it as a silky layer of natural sauce, as it is almost pure gelatine. Because it is the first part to cook, it sticks to your braai-grill or griddle if you don't oil it properly. It is also the first to shrink, and tear, unless you slash it handsomely. And it is also why burning will make it bitter, but gentle browning will enhance its caramelised deliciousness. Do not eat the skin or any other part of pufferfish (aka blaasop). It is deadly poisonous.

Because fish can exist near weightlessness in their dense water environment, they don't need the hardened gravity-fighting skeletons of land animals. Subsequently, these fragile bones yield their gelatine more willingly than our aforementioned oxtail. And it also, you will swiftly remind me, makes for more troublesome eating. But not with your new insight into the gelatine principle. Each side has a fillet lying on a

Mosidi Tsonye (aka Francina, Franci, Darling, Sweetheart, etc), KB's irreplaceable house manager and confidante since '94.

WHOLE FISH

grille-like backbone, right? And each fillet can be divided gently with a knife, where it is naturally separated on the spine, right? This lateral line can be seen on the skin, actually. Now, that bony grille has partially turned to slippery gelatine, and if you push the ¼ fillet away from the spine it will slip away effortlessly and await its boneless consumption.

So true is this, that it is a sure-fire test for doneness to pull the main spine of the dorsal fin, and if it comes out, that means the point where it was stuck in the thickest part has melted into gelatine. I am often horrified to witness fishmongers and (famous) chefs snip off the fins, leaving their roots treacherously embedded inside the flesh. They are extracted easily enough once cooked, and if crisped, are very, very tasty to the crunch.

Off you are, to your docile fishmonger, point at the freshest and prettiest plate-sized linefish, and with an air of suppressed superiority, instruct him to scale it only. Fins intact.

KitchArt in its most elevated & expensive guise. Each ingredient separately cast in resin and then dished up exactly as KB would serve whole fish.

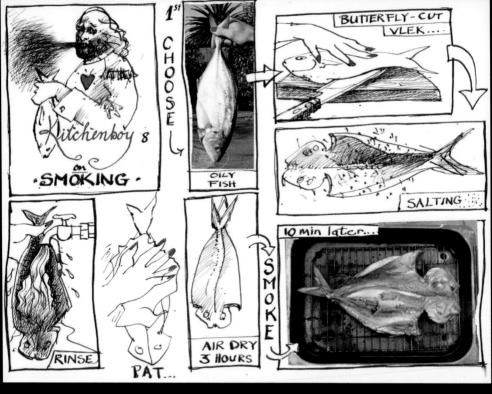

1st CHOOSE

Kitchenboy 8 on ·SMOKING·

OILY FISH

BUTTERFLY-CUT VLEK....

SALTING

10 min later...

RINSE

PAT...

AIR DRY 3 HOURS

SMOKE

Smoking fish & the difference between hot- or cold-smoking is much misunderstood among anglers. KB has converted more non-fish eaters with this than any other cooking method.

Two fine vlekked bonito drying in the draught of his hearth in The Chapel, a former KB abode.

SMOKED FISH

HOT-SMOKED FISH

Your modest, coughing, choking Kitchenboy is so adroit at the art of home-smoking fish, that he thinks he might have accidentally invented it himself in a former prehistoric lifetime, when he suspended his catch in the fumes of a campfire to keep the insects away.

First catch or hunt down an oily or fatty fish at your favourite fishmonger. With some exceptions, you will find the swift surface predators, the so-called gamefish, to have the oiliest flesh because of their fish diets. They can be distinguished by their aerodynamic bodies, small scales, retractable fins & deeply forked tails. A further test to determine this yourself is to run a finger over the open flesh and rub fingers as if asking for money; fatty fish will actually feel slippery/oily and sweet while non-oily flesh will feel watery. Contradictory as it may seem, wonderful white-fleshed tablefish like rockcod & kingklip are poor smokers. The seductive deliciousness of smoked food is directly related to the chemical reaction smoke has on animal fats: think of smoked ham, bacon, kippers, etc.

The best fish for smoking, in my personal order of preference, are all billfishes (marlin, sailfish), all tunas & mackerels (incl. king & queen), all kingfishes (incl. pompano, yellowtail, garrick), dolphinfish (aka dorado), salmon & trout, eel, snoek & butterfish (actually oilfish), sardine, elf (aka shad), 'angelfish' (actually pomfret), haarder (aka mullet) & sea barbel. Frozen fish will do, albeit at a stretch.

Ask your fishmonger to scale & butterfly or vlek your fish, i.e. split it open like a book, hinged by back or belly, leaving the tail to hang it by. Small whole fish, skin-on fillets or portions & thick steaks are cool

prevent it from tearing. The head can waai if you're squeamish or your smoker is too small, but you can see those eyes beg for it to go into a fish soup or stew. 'Wet fish don't smoke,' an old fisherman once told me, an understatement if ever there was one. I've met so many people who are disillusioned with their smokers, and almost without exception this was the golden rule they couldn't grasp. So let's go NB NB NB NB: The surface needs to be 'dry', or rather tacky, to give the smoke a kinda track to grip onto. This is easiest achieved by salting, ly salty tastes insipid and decidedly wrong. Salt the fish inside & out with, say, two or three handfuls of coarse salt, as I and most Orientals do anyway before cooking fish. Leave 30 minutes (less if small), and then rub all traces of salt off under RUNNING water. Pat utterly dry with paper towel or newspaper, and hang it by its tail in a cool draughty place, for about 3 hours. A skewer inside will prevent the sides from touching. The exposed surface flesh will develop a shiny skin (pellicle), tacky to your touch. Your fish is thus ready to smoke.

Robert Weinek, friend & owner of Bob's Bar in Troyeville, who persuaded KB to open a restaurant next door.

If the directions from here are rather vague, it is not so much that your fumigated Kitchenboy is stupid or stoned today, but because there are so many smoking contraptions on the market (he has at least 7). So follow the manufacturers' directions. Resinous sawdust (like pine) is considered harmful, so be sure to use commercial hardwood sawdust, it lasts forever and contains no insecticides. And use no more than 2 tbsp on a kg of fish, otherwise it will be bitter. Lay the fish skin-down on an oiled rack. A gas burner is most effective but some methylated spirit inventions work brilliantly. If the lid closes tightly, 10 minutes should be enough, timed from the moment the lid is too hot to touch (which indicates that steam is circulating inside and cooking the fish).

Home hot-smoking (which cooks the flesh), is NOT a preserving method like cold-smoking (which leaves the flesh raw & translucent), and hot-smoked food should be kept no longer than ordinary cooked food. But it is delicious all the same, dotted with butter while hot, with farm bread & red wine, beer or cider. Under an old oak tree. Hmmm.

Pst: Leftovers make brilliant pâté and are even better tossed in a vinaigrette with onions, peppers, garlic, mustard seeds & bay leaves.

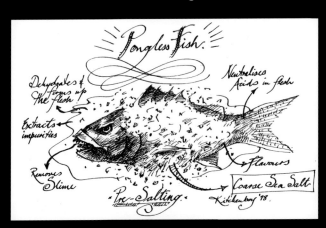

This pre-salting required for smoking also prevents pongs when cooked before drying. KB always does it.

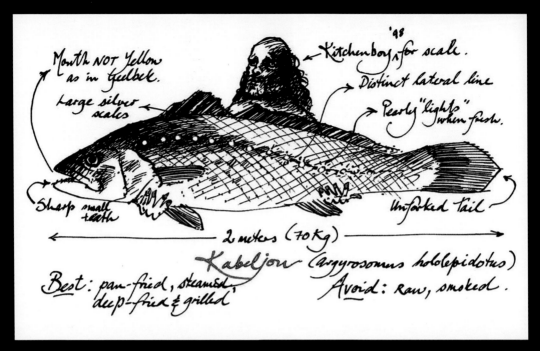

The drawing is annotated with the following handwritten notes:

'98

Mouth NOT Yellow as in Geelbek.

Kitchenboy for scale.

Large silver scales

Distinct lateral line

Pearly "lights" when fresh.

Sharp small teeth

Unforked tail

← 2 meters (70 kg) →

Kabeljou (argyrosomus hololepidotus)

Best: pan-fried, steamed, deep-fried & grilled

Avoid: Raw, smoked.

This is no exaggeration, kabeljou is by far the largest of our so-called tablefish.

Junglegirl's affinity for sarongs and KB's early fantasies of her thus wrapped, made it obligatory braai & pool-wear for visitors too.

~~KABELJOU~~

(ARGYROSOMUS HOLOLEPIDOTUS)

BLACKENED FISH

Blackened fish is the persistent favourite in the countless fish restaurants which now bless our country. So let your piscatorial Kitchenboy tell you about the fish that changed pan-frying forever, and how to make it at home, well then, outside home.

Few gourmets here realise that the Kabeljou family started that whole Cajun Blackened Fish craze in the 80s in the US, which brought their Redfish on the endangered list within a few years. Redfish belong to the Drum or Croaker family (so named because of the drumming or croaking sounds it emits when landed), and so do our own Kabeljou (aka Kob) and its two immediate relatives, the confusingly misnamed Cape Salmon (its real name being Geelbek) and the lesser-known Belman (aka Tasslefish & Baardman).

Big, fat and famous chef Paul Purdomme of New Orleans used slabs of fillet from this American redfish to reinvent this old regional cooking technique. Your sentimental Kitchenboy is always deeply touched by the heartbreaking resourcefulness of the poor, and this is yet another wonderful example of how their yearning for good food enriched the world with a magic dish. Historically, Blackened Fish is an outdoor cooking method invented by the Louisiana slaves to bully some taste into the bland and often muddy catfish they caught in the Mississippi River.

Monstrous kabeljou of 2 metres & 70 kg are not uncommon, though you are more likely to encounter half that size at your fishmonger. The most suitable cuts to ask for

KABELJOU

are tail-end steaks or fillets with the skin on (which keeps the flesh together), or whole (gutted & scaled only) when small enough to handle. A word of warning; never eat kabeljou or any of its family raw as in *sushi* or *sashimi*, they are notorious world-wide for harbouring harmful parasites.

This is a useful spice mix and your happy-go-lucky Kitchenboy sommer makes up a peanut-butter jar full of the stuff, hence the vague amounts. Make no mistake, it is equally fantastic on any other white-fleshed fish (kebab, fillet slab or steak) and superb with calamari & prawns. I am also very keen on dusting it before frying or baking, on chicken, pork or lamb, though preferably with stacks of garlic.

Fishmonger Willie Boshoff of George & KB with a monster, but not unusual, kabeljou

KABELJOU

BLACKENED KABELJOU

1 part black pepper, fine
1 part white pepper, fine
1 part cayenne pepper
3 parts paprika
1 part thyme, fine dried
1 part origanum, fine dried
2 parts salt
kabeljou fillets, portioned
butter to rub

NOTE: Some Americans add one part each of garlic salt & onion salt but food-snobs dismiss them as white-trash ingredients

- Come on, that's easy. Just chuck the dry bits together & mix.
- Then go OUTSIDE & heat a cast iron griddle plate till blisteringly hot.
- Meanwhile, rub the fillets with butter.
- Dust them heavily with your Cajun mix, if you dare.
- Slam it on the hot plate and duck for cover. It will smoke like mad, even catch fire and the volatile pepper oils will attack your lungs.
- Jaag back from cover after a minute or two, ducking & diving, to flip over the fillets with a spatula.
A dark red-brown-black crust of spices will have formed.
- Let them freak out further till almost cooked through and whip them off.
They will finish cooking on the trip to the table.
Serve with farm bread, beer and watermelon.
If your mouth is on fire, ja-a-a-a-a-a, use less spice mix next time.

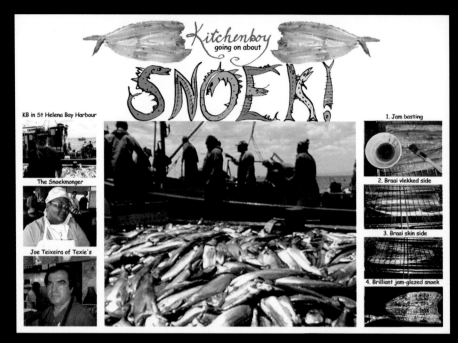

Kitchenboy going on about

SNOEK!

KB in St Helena Bay Harbour

The Snoekmonger

Joe Teixeira of Texie's

1. Jam basting

2. Braai vlekked side

3. Braai skin side

4. Brilliant jam-glazed snoek

St Helena Bay, one of many stops on the KB West Coast TV shoot. He was horrified at the brutal handling of the snoek. Sure, they were very dead already, but the oily, fragile flesh was devastatingly bruised.

'99 12 31

Ever since setting his romantic sights & hopes on Junglegirl, KB dreamed of marrying her on the turn of the Millennium. She obliged him with this magical play-ceremony at exactly midnight on New Year's Eve.

SNOEK

SNOEK & APRICOT JAM

Your landlocked Kitchenboy wasn't just a little chuffed when Cape Talk Radio producer, Tama Khan, phoned him in Johannesburg to inform Capetonians what to do with the glut of snoek in the city, eh eh he. They surfaced at Granger Bay, where they were sold that early evening for a song.

Snoek are of the snake mackerel family (*Gempylidae*), but to our typical perplexity, the Dutch named it after the ferocious fresh-water pike (snook) in Holland. Inexplicably, the flesh of some individuals are pap or mealy, as many as 5 in 100. Fishermen told me this happens when its neck is incorrectly broken, either under the arm or between the legs (not by meeeeee). Their fearsome bite possesses an anticoagulant, reme-died by squeezing a snoek's eye onto the wound, lest you bleed yourself kis into the sea. Such is the lore and superstition in the wake of our national and ideal braai fish.

A langana (middleman/whole-saler/smous) showed me how a prime snoek should be flexible, and he duly whipped it about to prove his point. 'Once it has gone stiff (rigor mortis), it is tickets, it goes pap', he said. Ag sweet, man, but, it's more likely their insane handling of the catch, the weight borne by the first ones caught, laying under the others in the bakke while out at sea in the sun for hours. I was dismayed to see the fish flung from boat to pier in huge piles in St Helena Bay harbour. If only they knew how easily oily fish bruise and thus deteriorate. So, as with most foods, choose a handsome, shiny fish with unblemished skin.

traditionally, snoek are vlekked, which is very different to butterfly-ing, and as far as I know, unique to our shores. Beheaded and then slit open from the back (next to the dorsal fin), the 2 sides are hinged by the belly. Then a 3rd flap (the backbone) is cut, and it is this piece that is my most favourite, whether braaied or smoked, eaten like corn on the cob. Before cooking, the flesh is greatly improved by mild curing (see recipe). Important to remember though, is to omit this step if using frozen snoek, since most commercial fisheries salt them before freezing. I may add that this is also the preparation if you wish to smoke it, but be sure to hang it up after rinsing to dry for a few hours before smoking.

Along the wine farming Cape coast the snoek run follows the harvesting and subsequently, home-made moskonfyt (grape-must jam) and borriepatats (those dryish yel-low sweet potatoes) make up the symphony of their regional snoek-braai. But on my recent visit to the wine-barren West Coast, I found this charming folk recipe. Don't be put off by the trashy apricot jam, it makes perfect sense as a sweet glaze (as for a whole ham), and becomes lusciously sweet-sour when juiced up with lemon at table.

Much to our partners' credit, nothing diminished the very special relationship between KB & lead-ing friendgirl, Nicole Abel.

SNOEK

SNOEK & APRICOT JAM

2 cups coarse salt

BASTING
2 tbsp butter
2 tbsp apricot jam
3 cloves garlic, chopped
fresh red chilli, chopped (or plenty black pepper)

1 fresh snoek, vlekked
oil for the grill
lemons for serving

- Salt the fish generously and after 20 min,
rinse thoroughly under running cold water.
- Pat dry with newspaper or paper towel.
- Melt the basting ingredients together in a saucepan
or the microwave.
- Oil a hinged grill and the skin-side of the snoek.
- Paint the flesh-side only with the baste, clamp,
and braai this side first till golden brown.
- Flip over and slowly cook from skin-side till barely cooked through.

Kitchenboy in PERU

Equestrian paintings have always captivated KB, as have cliffs, rivers & bridges. This was done during the state of emergency, and he has vowed that all his artworks will feature Johannesburg burning in the background until it has been lifted.

Effervescent & exquisite Juanine Bouwer, close friend of JG and now of KB, during a boisterous reunion at her new abode.

PERU

ACID-COOKING FISH

Whether from Parys-Vereeniging to Paris-France, from Koekenaap to Saigon or St Lucia to Nagasaki, gastronomy must be the cheapest way of flying. Thus your flamboyant Kitchenboy mounted his culinary stallion and crossed the Jukskei to Peru-Pretoria, at a sumptuous dinner on the pool deck of the new Sheraton Hotel, overlooking the floodlit Union Buildings on Meintjieskop.

Dressed to the teeth for our imminent hobnobbing with Latin American diplomats, my darling friendgirl (as in girlfriends one dare not sleep with), the gorgeous actress Nicole Abel & I tucked straight into the spirit of Peru with a series of Pisco Sours. It is the deceivingly delicious national cocktail concocted with Quebranta *pisco*, a fiery grape brandy (not unlike our witblits), lemon juice, egg white & cinnamon. This one courtesy of the Embassy of Peru.

PISCO SOUR
1 cup Quebranta *pisco*
½ cup lemon juice
½ cup white sugar
1 egg white
6 ice cubes

ground cinnamon
Flash-blend ingredients in a blender.
Strain into chilled champagne flutes.
Sprinkle a little ground cinnamon on top.

High as a kite, our distinctly foreign sojourn started with *Anticochos de Corazo*n, a robust streetfood-sosatie of marinated ox heart with a pungently scrumptious chilli sauce, followed by a spread of liberating regional dishes which had us soaring over the Andes, the Amazon and the Pacific coastline. But a dish I have always been fascinated with, is Peruvian *cebiche*, of which many versions exist all over Latin America, variously called *seviche*, *ceviche* and other corruptions of the Mediterranean Arabic word *sebech*, meaning acidic food.

The preparation of it is a most misunderstood cooking technique, if you could call it that in the absence of fire. When meat or fish is cooked, the protein is denatured and changes from translucent to opaque, and this is exactly what it amounts to when fish or seafood is marinated in lemon juice. If your abhorrence of raw meat needs further encouragement, think of all those baddies in horror flicks, who get so seriously fried when acid is thrown in their faces.

Many Peruvians believe God is Peruvian and *cebiche* an act of God, and they despise the wannabe *cebiches* of other cultures where the fish is acid-cooked for hours into a flaccid mess. Purists insist that super-fresh fish needs only a few minutes marinating in the lemon juice, a little garlic, salt, fresh chilli and it should be eaten immediately. A travel guide from 1866 describes the spicy dishes of Peru, 'but the hottest of spicy dishes, which causes more tears to be shed (after jealousy) is the *cebiche*.' Of the many indigenous chillies (*ají*) of Peru, the small but explosive hot *ají limo* (ribs & seeds removed), is much loved.

The classic *cebiche* is made with corvina (of the kabeljou family) but any other sweet non-oily fish like rock cod, red roman and sole could be used, as well as shellfish like prawn, calamari, perlemoen, octopus, clams, sea urchins and, stupendously, scallops.

KB & Grethe Fox as Adam & Eve, on the closed side-panels of the *Justitia Triptych*. She was a fabulous & patient model and left many artworks in her wake.

PERU

PERUVIAN CEBISCE

1 kg fresh non-oily fish fillets or shellfish
freshly squeezed lemon juice (to cover fish)
1 clove garlic, chopped
4/5 fresh small red chillies (chopped & seeded)
1 red onion, sliced
fresh coriander leaves
salt

- Slice the fish, season with salt, pepper & chilli.
- Cover with lemon juice, add garlic & stand for 30 minutes.
- Garnish with onion & coriander leaves & serve with slices of cooked corn on the cob.

Understandably overdressed & wobbly from the Pisco Sours, Nicole & I hit the Pretoria night club circuit with a vengeance till 4 in the morning, which was as foreign and exhilarating an experience as one can have from this side of the Jukskei River.

An actor's actor and one of the most focused minds of contemporary theatre, Amanda Lane is highly esteemed & adored by KB. At her birthday party.

This camp memory drawing, based on her childhood yearning to be Sheena, Queen of the Jungle, and the tropical vegetation of St Lucia, coined Junglegirl's pseudonym.

KB & Junglegirl on their studio couch during her first visit, to cautiously check out the lay of the land.

south, and dumped my body in Dullstroom, but I was promptly entangled in scandalous weekend behaviour with the far too many people I knew, or who knew me.

So after a dreary breakfast I sneaked out of town and ambled southwards.

The harsh winter left its scorched landscapes behind me as I drove though a William Kentridge charcoal along the backroads to nowhere. Descending on the lowlands of Pongola, with its papayas, palm trees, bougainvilleas and sugar cane fields, I began to tingle with a sense of destination, which lay ahead where the thick clouds were condensing from the Indian Ocean.

A balmy, laid back holiday resort in a tropical jungle with palms, enormous trees adorned with dense climbers and monkey vines, exactly as Thomas Baines painted them, and an awesome variety of every conceivable living species in the St Lucia Wetlands Park, deservedly declared a World Heritage Site. Nonetheless, I was fully intent on leaving the next day. But that was not to be, and des- tined to change my future life for- ever. Quite innocently, honestly, I befriended a gangly, carefree young local girl and her boyfriend. We partied relentlessly, fished on the estuary, braaied & dined in the tourist restaurants (where they worked) and talked the nights away on the beach. It was only when I drove out of the town three weeks later, that I painfully realised that I was now an incomplete person. A romance was born and after an intense longdistance courtship, she finally moved into my life to become my precious Junglegirl, with whom I have been enchanted ever since. Intrigued by her lovely person, but not remotely expecting my hedonistic bachelor ways to change so radically, even though all the ingredients were already on the table, I created & named this dish for her. It needs to be explained that Junglegirl could never go to sleep before she witnessed the sun rising over the sea, even when it was raining. To tease & charm her, I used only everyday local produce like grunter, pineapples & the curious guavadilla.

KB has charmed, flirted with and made love to many woman through food, but never intended or expected the outcome of this dish.

~~ST LUCIA~~

JUNGLEGIRL'S JUNGLE DAWN FISH
WITH PINEAPPLE-GUAVADILLA SAUCE

1 litre pineapple juice
1 cup cider vinegar
1 cup sugar
1 tot dark rum
1 thumb fresh ginger (cut in matchsticks)
1½ cups guavadilla pulp (or grenadilla)
10 bird's eye chillies, chopped
1 small pineapple, cut in wedges
2 sweet peppers, red, yellow & green, cut in strips

4 small whole linefish (600-800 g), de-scaled only
cornflour for dusting
oil for panfrying

4 wild strelitzia leaves for serving
1½ cups roasted pecan nuts
hibiscus flowers for tropical dekorasie

- In a large saucepan, boil then simmer the pineapple juice, cider vinegar, sugar, guavadilla pulp, ginger & chilli to infuse and reduce till syrupy. Add pineapple & peppers just before serving, to heat through.
- Dust whole, de-scaled fish in cornflour and fry in a skottel-skaar braai-thingy, or any other which way you like. Yeah, even battered fillets or nuggets. Drain on paper but don't bother to keep warm. It's warm enough here. Anyway, don't be so obsessed with hot food.
- Place the fish on a small wild strelitzia or banana leaf & tumble the whole shebang over the fish.
- Scatter pecan nuts over & decorate with hibiscus or bougainvillea flowers
- Serve with green banana and *amadumbi* chips dusted with masala. Or plain unsalted rice. NOT Tastic.

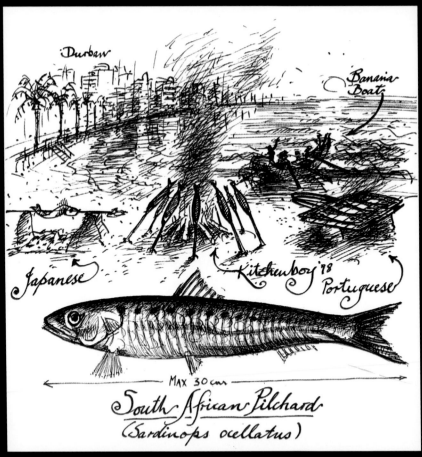

Durban

Banana Boatz

Japanese

Kitchenboy '98

Portuguese

MAX 30 cm

South African Pilchard
(Sardinops ocellatus)

Sardine was never a favourite fish of KB, not before he had a fresh one. It is well worth the trip to Durban during the annual sardine run. Besides, tacky Durb's has a weird & pleasurable impact on his psyche.

Director Pieter Cilliers gets the dubious credit for discovering KB as a TV cook.

~~SARDINES~~

SARDINE BEACH BRAAI

There he was, your bewildered Kitchenboy, ready to throw up in the wind. Trapped against a pile of fishy wet beach seine nets on the stern of a goofy banana boat, with an irate skipper hollering at his inexperience, and another fisherman on top of him, frenetically scooping out leaking seawater with an old pot. My director/cameraman Slowmo (everyone at Kitchenboy has nicknames), is perching laconically on the bobbing bow, zooming in on your green presenter, who feigns worldly calm as he speaks nonchalantly on the perils of trekking sardines in an ancient rowing skiff. The Fairy, his trusted gourmet guide, is far away, ashore, beside herself with mirth. Clearly, this crew is making the pre-eminent video on procuring and understanding South African sea fish.

Durban must be one of my most favourite cities. Maybe just because it is a port city, and a handsome one at that, with its palm-lined streets and colonial buildings. Perhaps because I am so secretly attracted to its seedy side with sailors' nightclubs & hookers, for something deliciously devious surfaces when I'm there. I am fascinated too by the aimlessly wandering tourists from Gauteng and the migrating homeless flocking after the dank and humid sunshine. And I dearly love the downtown curry dens where our national convenience food, the bunny chow, was born.

But the real attraction is probably the bustling Indian Quarter around Grey Street with its cantankerous Victoria Street Fish Market, arguably the most brilliant in Africa. 'R5-a-dozen' yodels the owner of a battered bakkie, parked at the entrance in Fishmarket Street. It is brimful with hour-old sardines, still crumbed with sea sand from its landing at Addington Beach. So we jaag over there in my Kitchmobile, with whining sirens, to record the action of the annual sardine run every April.

SARDINES

As we arrive, the trek-nets are again being hauled onto the beach. Traditionally those bystanders who help trekking are entitled to a couple of fish, which is how I too get a few sardines, as young pilchards are called. Handle them with care, for their rich oily flesh is incredibly fragile, manifested by the many fallen fish squashed barefoot into the soft sand.

It is exactly this oiliness which renders them perfect for braaiing, for they require no basting at all. It is also no coincidence that they are invariably cooked out of doors, because their aroma and smoke is a mighty fishy one. And please note that sardines are not traditionally gutted & beheaded. You just munch it hand-&-teeth like a little mealie, around the ribcage. The flesh comes away from the fine hair-bones with ease, even for a novice, and its crisply toasted skin is eminently edible too.

The Portuguese, who practically invented sardine-cuisine, first salt their sardines heavily with coarse salt for an hour or so, to firm up

Producer Angela McClelland started KB's long relationship with Radio 702

SARDINES

the flesh. Then they shake off the salt and braai them in a hinged grill till golden. I also like salt-grilling them the Japanese way, to thread them head-first onto a rod, sort of zigzag, in a swimming position, which makes for a spectacular, if minimalist, presentation. Also no basting here, but a trick worth remembering is the fine salt they pinch onto only the wet fragile fins before they braai it. This prevents them from charring. Then support the skewer between two rocks or bricks, straddling glowing coals, and turn till blistered & done.

But as your cunning Kitchenboy impulsively licked the metallic skin of a sardine after he rinsed the sand off in the sea, it hit on him that here they were already salty enough to braai as is. So he impaled them through the mouth onto sharpened sticks and planted them into the beach, at a 60° angle, in a ritual circle around a blazing fire. And grilled them so to bronze perfection in the intense radiated heat.

Jeremy Mansfield, then with Radio 702, anchored KB's weekly live food slot on his Saturday afternoon show. He was rampant, provocative and great fun to work with during those few years.

Margarine Peacock with Mortadella & Olives was painted in exchange for a week at a luxury resort on Mauritius, and teased their overdressed old French cuisine parading as local Creole food. Little did KB realise what a powerful influence it would have on his later food career.

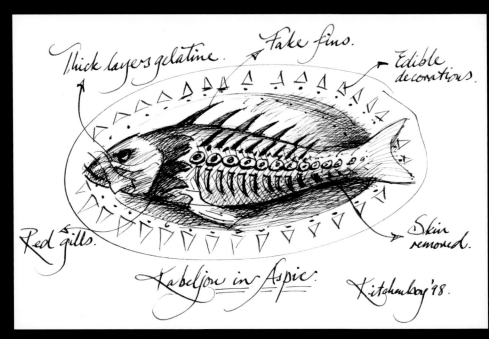

When living in Antwerp as a penniless young artist, KB stared hungrily at a skinned trout, decorated with tarragon & black truffles, glazed in aspic. It was too beautiful to be real, like a plastic toy. This was designed for a feature in Elle.

KABELJOU IN ASPIC

There goes your troubled old Kitchenboy again, missioning off onto his imaginary palm-fringed island, moaning and mumbling along. Hot and balmy climates, so bountiful that a man would grow where you planted a foot in the self-mulching soil. Where lunch or dinner would be had in the shade at air temperature.

I could never come to grips with what I call the SA Hot-tray Syndrome, a hangover from the electric carving knife days, in our enviably outdoor-perfect country. Bad enough that we play rugby in jerseys and spray the shopwindows full of fake snow over the summer holidays. But why do we insist on having hot food on a perfect day? The European heritage bears some of the blame, what with all that animal fat we still cook with, but hey, let's get real about living in Africa; that was three and a half centuries ago.

We should allow ourselves to be cued by other sun-belt regions where the cuisine is dictated by the local weather conditions. Think of the lazing *tapas* and the *mezze* of Mediterranean countries, of the fresh *salsas* instead of reduced sauces in Latin America, the dainty spreads of exquisite room-temperature dishes of South East Asia and, close to my kitsch gourmet heart, the garish cold buffet displays of tropical island hotels.

My accompanying painting was commissioned by a hotel on Mauritius and represents the French/Creole cuisine peculiar to those resorts. You don't quite have to go the way of the Chilled Margarine Peacock decorated with Mortadella & Olives (ice-sculpture gone seriously wrong), but the red and black decorated cold aspic (gelatine) fish in the foreground is beautiful food at its breathtaking best. Secretly, your playful Kitchenboy likes it because it parades as plastic toy-food for grownups. Surprisingly, it is frightfully simple to prepare, even if it may take you a while, but we're talking about laying on a feast, right? Even the day before. And this showy center-piece for your next pool or dinner party will certainly stimulate the frustrated artist within you to new heights.

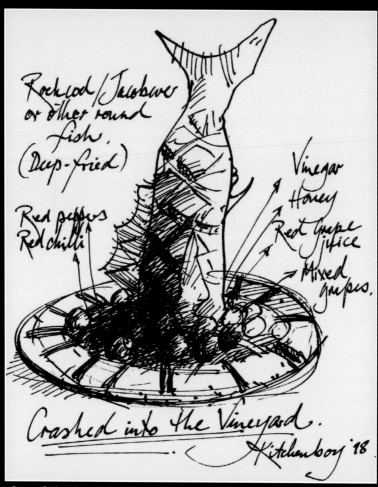

Rock cod / Jacobiver or other round fish. (Deep-fried)

Red peppers Red chilli

Vinegar Honey Red Grape juice Mixed grapes.

Crashed into the Vineyard.

Kitchenboy '18

One of the drawbacks of initiating dishes with a drawing and expanding from there, as is KB's custom, is that it rarely resembles the final thing. With black grapes, red grape juice & a fish too big for the plate in hand, he boldly predicted the marvel of his invention on TV & lopped the head off. But he didn't reckon with the shrinkage of the flesh, and the backbone protruded like a spike, so he secretly tucked wads of paper under the fish to make it stand up.

TROPICAL CUISINE

KABELJOU IN ASPIC

THE FISH
1 large, whole kabeljou
(or 4/6 small whole linefish)
coarse salt

THE ASPIC
1½ envelopes (6 tsp) unflavoured gelatine
½ cup cold water
2 cups canned chicken consommé
¼ cup cognac
1 tbsp lemon juice

THE DECORATIONS
red, green, yellow peppers & chillies
glacé cherries and carrots
olives, fresh herbs like tarragon (anything edible, actually)

- Liberally salt the fish in and out, and let stand for 20 minutes.
- Rinse the salt off & pat dry. • Oil a double sheet of foil and place into a bamboo steamer or large roasting pan with a rack. If too big for the steamer, cut the head off to reassemble afterwards. • Cover and steam till cooked through. • Very carefully, lift the fish out of steamer and place on the presentation platter. Once done it cannot be moved.
- Peel the skin off from shoulder to tail and carefully pull out the dorsal, anal & pectoral fins. • Now chill completely to firm up.
- Meanwhile, rain the gelatine on the cold water and let it sit, while you heat the consommé and cognac through. • Add soft gelatine and stir till dissolved. • Add lemon juice and chill till syrupy. Remember gelatine must never boil. • Cut the dekorasies in pretty shapes. Dip them in aspic and decorate the entire fish and the plate. • Carefully paint layers of gelatine over fish, waiting for each to set, till it is coated with a thick, glossy glaze. • Chill till served.

During his early years as an artist, KB lived on & learned to cook with inexpensive chick-
en, never tired of it & never realised how sexy they were till he painted this one. But few
cooks realise what a health hazard they can pose.

~~CHICKEN~~

LAZY ARTIST'S ROAST CHICKEN & GINGER-SOY STEAMED CHICKEN

In a former lifetime as a starving bachelor artist, your scheming Kitchenboy quickly discovered the culinary glories of the obliging chicken. Jislaaik, you could buy a whole chicken for a rand back then, throw a bring-your-own dinner party for four eccentrics and get schloshed and lucky in the process. Indeed, one could say that chickens taught him to cook fearlessly.

When I then painted this picture of a plucked chicken, I was startled by the features bridging the evolutionary gap between dinosaurs & humankind, almost a contrived genetically engineered hoax. Reptile beak, unblinking eyes and a shrill tongue. Even the blades on a dinosaur's back, used to regulate their body temperature (by turning it to or against the sun), are echoed in a cock's comb, the very reason it clambers onto a pole to heat up in the first rays of the morning. But it is those blerrie scaled & clawed legs which get to me. The muscles in between these extremities I frequently see at the local gym. But by 2000 BC it was the inhabitant of the Indus valley, who domesticated their Red Jungle Fowl (*Gallus gallus*), identified by Darwin as the ancestor of our modern plaashoender. It is no small accident that Indians today, and people of other humid countries, still prefer cooking chickens stripped of their skins.

Chicken with skin contain 10 000 times more bacteria per square centimetre than any other meat we eat, with a terrifying 10 000-fold population increase during six days in your fridge. At your next function or wedding, give those ominous drumsticks a miss. There is only one way of buying a chicken: smell it. Tear the clingwrap at the pope's nose end and if you smell anything, walk away and alert the supermarket manager.

CHICKEN

As with all birds. God never intended the lean breasts & sinewy legs to be cooked together. Breast meat is white in chicken because they are hardly used these days, and do not require red oxygen-storing myoglobin as found in the almost black pigeon breast muscle, and they contain very little fat. That is why many cooks stuff herb butter into the bra-pocket under the skin, or cover the breast with foil. leaves or bacon. Even so, bet on overdone breasts. To test chicken for done-ness, poke a gaatjie into the thick thigh and see clear (not pink) juice running out. If nothing oozes out, throw away & start again. Okay, okay, some people still eat it. but don't invite me.

These two recipes are childishly simple, but believe me, as good as it gets.

All the tables in KB's restaurant were painted by him. So were the chairs, which featured the naked bottoms of mixed gender. this one covered by a box of chillies. It certainly wasn't a place for sissies.

~~CHICKEN~~

LAZY ARTIST'S ROAST CHICKEN

1 very fresh medium free-range chicken (with skin)
oil or butter
salt
pepper

- Remove any lappies or plastic bags in the chicken,
and remove excess fat. • Dab dry with paper towel
- Rub entire outside with butter or oil. This will crisp the skin.
- Rub generously with salt & pepper. • Lie it on its back in a roasting
pan and slam it into an oven @ 200 °C (400 °F) for 45 minutes.
Puncture to test. • Go 10 more minutes if juices are still pink.
- Rest a little before serving.

GINGER-SOY STEAMED CHICKEN

1 very fresh medium free-range chicken, skinless
½ cup good soy sauce (Kikkoman)
½ cup shredded fresh ginger

- Place chicken in a deep bowl to catch the cooking juices.
- Pour soy sauce over it and rain ginger shreds on top. • Put a rack or
upturned saucer inside a pot with 2 fingers of water. • Place the bowl
with chicken thereon. • Cover tightly with a lid and steam briskly for an
hour. • Transfer chicken to deep plate, pour juices over and cool first to
room temperature & then refrigerate till juices jellify.
- Steal torn pieces for 2 days from fridge or serve cold slivers with
the jelly, wrapped in little pancakes.

Kitchenboy sikelele iAfrica

This large painting was started after seeing the film *Gorillas in the Mist*. KB has always had an attraction to Hollywood versions of the African jungle.

A guide of the Johannesburg Art Gallery told him that school children would stare deep into the picture and wave back at the tiny figure of Jane/Tarzana/Junglegirl.

AFRICA

CHICKEN OR GUINEA FOWL IN PEANUT SOUP

For no frivolous reason has your whitewashed Kitchenboy taken his name from his African ancestors, the forgotten chefs among the derogatorily named 'houseboys' of colonial kitchens.

It hurts him deeply to see his continent's image depicted as one of greedy despots, begging famished children, civil wars & barbarism. He believes it is the last of the great cuisines of the world waiting to be discovered and explored. It is time to wake up; to take stock of who we are and where we come from. One of my greatest discoveries was the milk extracted from the West African palmnut, more or less what coconut milk is to South-East Asia, and retrieved in much the same way. It has a glowing orange colour and gorgeous flavour and is the basis for the brilliant national dish of the Congo, Chicken Moambe. But the bright yellow palmnut oil is much used for frying, also enjoyed by many local Portuguese, and has a pungency which is an acquired taste, to say the least.

The cassava plant (aka manioc or yuka), originally from South America, is extensively used in West Africa for its leaves & tubers. The leaves are cooked as a vegetable, often flavoured with smoked baby catfish from the Congo River. The tubers are cooked to rid it of its poison and eaten whole or pounded into another form of *fufu*. In the Congo this mush is fermented, tightly wrapped in cassava leaves and steamed into a national delicacy, called *kwanga*, a curious evasively sour, chewy staple sausage. The tubers are also ground into a par-boiled grainy meal *(gari)*, which you simply cover with boiling water. Let it stand for 15 minutes and fluff it with a fork like couscous. *Fufu* proper is made from a fine pure-white flour, and it demands quite some dexterity of the cook to get it perfectly smooth. I have often watched it being made but never managed to crack the technique. Pity, since I am hooked on it. Traditionally a ball of *fufu* is placed on a soup and thus eaten with wet fingers, an alarming thought at first, but bear in mind that the gluey *fufu* is a breast-textured ball which won't let go of your hand when eaten any other way. It greatly pleases the gourmet in me to witness the enrichment of our collective culture with the new availability of these foreign ingredi-ents – first on the streets where illegal homesick immigrants do their shopping, and then in official African delis. Why, I have even bought steaming packets of boiled cassava tubers from a roadside stall near Hoedspruit.

Guinea fowl, the wild fowl of Africa, and peanuts feature in tandem as soups & stews all over Africa, like this unctuous soup from Ghana, Sierra Leone and Mali. It is sometimes thickened with indigenous okra (aka *gombo*, whence the gumbos of Louisiana). Use chicken by all means, though I made this one with the flavourful dark flesh of a wily old tarentaal, a gift from my old Bushveld-love, Wimpie.

Oh Isabella, beautiful but tempestuous ex-girlfriend, who moved into the restaurant with KB after its closure.

AFRICA

NKATENKWAN
GUINEA FOWL OR CHICKEN PEANUT SOUP

1 guinea fowl or chicken, portioned
2 tbsp oil
2 onions, sliced
3 large tomatoes, peeled (or 1 can)
2 litres chicken stock
1 cup ground, roasted peanuts (or peanut butter)
6 whole chillies (or to taste)
salt

• Brown the fowl in oil & remove. • Glaze the onions, add tomato, cook a little & purée. • Add chicken stock, stir in peanut paste until dissolved. • Add whole chillies & salt. • Simmer till fowl is tender, remove meat & chillies. • Boil soup fast to thicken, stirring. Beware, peanuts burn easily. • Return meat whole or shredded.
• Traditionally served with a ball of *fufu* & eaten with soup-wet fingers. • Replace it with a ball of soft mieliepap, as they too sometimes do.

Guinea Fowl fired in Clay, during a TV sketch at Phinda Game reserve. KB was amused to bits by decorating it like the curios sold on the roadside.

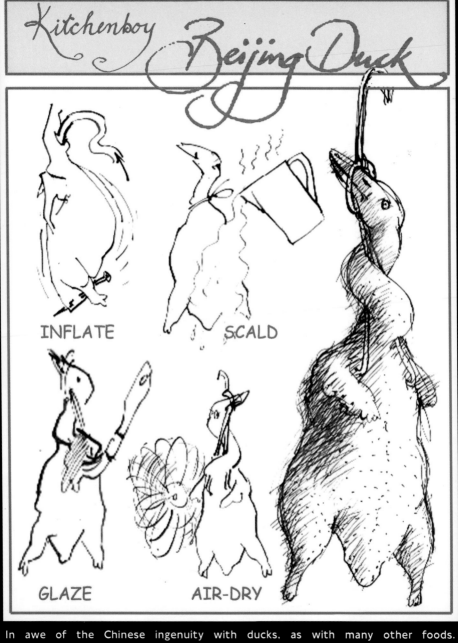

Kitchenboy Beijing Duck

INFLATE

SCALD

GLAZE

AIR-DRY

In awe of the Chinese ingenuity with ducks, as with many other foods.
Once, before Christmas, the truck delivering the ducks was hijacked with its
entire cargo. It nearly brought Chinatown to its knees.

BEIJING DUCK

BEIJING DUCK & MANDARIN PANCAKES

When you are a pompous culinary buffoon, like your gatskop Kitchenboy, you are perpetually asked what you rate as the greatest dish of all centuries. His tired old hooded eyes would light up, and he would whisper wickedly: 'Beijing Duck', as he relives the most delirious marriage & balance of flavours ever created, the crisp lacquered skin, moist breast meat, spring onion & hoisin sauce, wrapped in a curiously bland pancake.

I also venerate it for its lush history, culture and demanding dedication to prepare. Traditionally it should be served as 3 courses. First the above, then a stir-fry of the dark meat and finally, a soup made of the carcass, which gives one an endearing understanding of the frugal Chinese inclination to serve a soup at the end of a meal.

Dear friend Ken Sue, owner of Dajung supermarket, taught KB much about Chinese foods, and caused his drift away from European cooking towards the East. Part of KB's installation on the fringe of the Johannesburg Biennial, where he rotated different ethnic foods hanging from a chandelier. The container got so hot that this duck rotted in no time, to the horror of the press.

~~BEIJING DUCK~~

BEIJING DUCK
(Formerly known as Peking Duck)

1 whole duck (Chinese cut or other)
2 tbsp maltose or honey
1 cup hot water

- First inflate the duck to separate the skin from the meat.
This will render the skin very crisp, which is the aim. I use a bicycle or lilo-pump but any other will do. If using a proper Chinese duck with head on, skewer and/or hold the bottom gap as airtight as possible.
- Insert a pump nozzle in the neck incision and inflate; tie string around neck to trap air. If an ordinary duck, massage skin to loosen a little and attempt the same.
- Holding the duck by the neck on a hook or string, pour or ladle boiling water over repeatedly to tighten the skin.
- Pat dry and hang up till dry to the touch, about 4 hours (an electric fan will halve this time).
- Dissolve the maltose or honey in the cup of hot water and paint onto the entire duck.
- Hang to dry again. They are hung on eccentric hooks by the Chinese (see pic).

In Beijing the ducks are hung & roasted in special brick ovens with fragrant wood and locally, in wacky stainless steel tub ovens fired by gas, but I get near authentic results in a preheated electric oven @ 200 °C (400 °F). Lay the duck on its back on a rack in a roasting pan. Duck sizes vary, but I invariably cook them for exactly an hour, aiming for a dark red crackling skin, even at the expense of drying the meat a little.

BEIJING DUCK

MANDARIN PANCAKES
(aka Peking Doilies)

2¼ cups flour
less than 1 cup boiling water
sesame oil

• Chuck flour into processor & pour boiling water slowly,
till a firm ball forms around the shaft. • Cling-wrap for 30 minutes.
• Roll into sausage & cut into equal discs. • Flatten with palm, paint one side
with sesame oil & sandwich with another piece. • Roll out into a saucer-sized
circle with a rolling pin or tortilla press. • Grill both sides on a griddle plate
till coloured. • Separate the 2 pancakes. • Repeat. • Steam or microwave
to reheat when serving.

TO SERVE
Beijing duck
spring onion
cucumber
hoisin sauce
mandarin pancakes

• Remove the entire skin & cut into small rectangles. • Cut all the meat
into bite-size pieces and arrange skin and meat decoratively on a large
platter. • Cut the spring onion into pinkie-lengths & shred lengthways.
• De-seed & cut cucumber into chunky julienne strips. • Arrange
them on another platter with quarter-folded pancakes and a small bowl
of hoisin sauce. Each guest spreads a little sauce on the pancake, followed
by a piece of skin, meat, spring onion & cucumber. • Fold it over like a
spring roll and close your eyes when you deserve the first bite.

The Beauty & the Beast, St George & the Dragon and other such opposites in style &
content are reflected in both KB's art and his food. The one enhances the other.

The truth behind this half-cured & toasted duck breast is that KB intended to make biltong, but
had 2 days left before a function, leaving the fat & skin perfectly raw. So he had to find
a way to cook the fat only.

~~DUCK BREASTS~~

HALF-CURED TOASTED DUCK BREAST

Ja, ja, okay. So your gallivanting Kitchenboy has been around lately. Jirre, if only you could see him hosting cookouts and hobnobbing with world-famous chefs in Cape Town, featuring in glossy magazine spreads, cooking lavish designer banquets for VIPs, starring in TV ads and videos, launching his personal range of sauces, doing radio shows on 702 & Cape Talk, reviewing restaurants and so on and so forth.

The terrific thing about such intensive proximity to all things food – as well as pressure to perform – is that one is forced to think on one's feet, make flash decisions, improvise and invent solutions. Thus came this duck breast thing I want to share with you.

Duck breast must be one of the most luxurious meats available: simultaneously lean & rich, the dark gamy flesh is covered with a thick layer of prize fat, and invariably exorbitantly priced. Duck & geese also take admirably to smoking & curing, as in the French *Confit de Canard*. Chef Eric Springer once served me a magnificent *Duck ham*, duck breasts rolled in a tight cylinder in muslin and slow-cured over 3 weeks.

When I recently cured breasts for an extravagant dinner for 20 in my mansion, I found the duck to be at its prime after 2 or 3 days: tender, moist and delicious. Trouble was, the fat & skin were still practically raw. So I hit on the idea of cooking the fat only by pressing it onto a very hot griddle for under a minute, toasting the skin to crisp crackling, and rendering much of the fat out. The result was a heavenly dance of flavours, alternating between duck, wet biltong, bacon and toasted spices. By the way, my darling kosher gourmets, this blows that hilarious *makin* (fake chicken bacon) right out of the water.

DUCK BREASTS

The Chinese business community fled the rampant crime in Old Chinatown in the city centre and resettled in a quiet street in Cyrildene, turning it into a bustling New Chinatown with ever-changing restaurants & supermarkets. KB has always been a champion of the marginalised ethnic food beats, and has done much to popularise this fascinating neighbourhood.

~~DUCK BREASTS~~

KITCHENBOY'S
HALF-CURED TOASTED DUCK BREAST

2 duck breasts (with fat)
3 tbsp balsamic vinegar
3 heaped tbsp coarse salt
1 tbsp black peppercorns
½ tsp allspice (aka Jamaican pepper)
2 cloves
1 heaped tbsp coriander seed
½ tsp dried origanum (or 2 tsp fresh)

• Defrost breasts if frozen. Do not wash. Blot dry. • Lay them in an acid-proof tray & rub thoroughly with balsamic vinegar. • Sprinkle salt on both sides. • Grind or pound spices & rub everything deep into both sides. • Leave flesh-down, cover with cling wrap & leave to cure overnight in fridge (about 8 hrs). Turn a few times if you're an insomniac. • Shake & wipe all salt away by hand. Blot absolutely dry with paper, even pressing a little. • Hang by hook or string in a cool, draughty place, away from pets, pests & gourmets. You can speed this up with a fan or heater placed underneath. • Leave 2 days, till flesh forms a shiny black skin (pellicle). • Score the fat in narrow grooves. • Place skin-down on a hot griddle plate, one at a time, pressing down to cook & release fat and form a crisp, golden crust. Watch closely, the fat will turn translucent. Do not let the flesh cook. • Blot to remove fat & cool in fridge. • Slice paper-thin slivers and serve as carpaccio, *sashimi* or, best of all, on a salad platter with decorative fruit with your own or Kitchenboy's Girlfriend Dressing (see page 30).

Psst: When the breasts haven't been air-dried, the fat won't score. It slips around on the flesh like a loose-fitting nylon panty. So scoring will look shitty.

This painting, sans pigeon, a pun on a picture by Chagall, *Man with Seven Fingers*, was commissioned by Chagall's Restaurant of Pretoria, where KB had his 1st *Pigeon Breast Carpaccio*. A worker who saw it being installed, commented:" Jisses, but he sukkeled with the hands, hey ..."

Tarzan lived on the roof of the restaurant and of KB's '54 Chev, permanently parked outside. Actually, he owned the street ...

BROTHS VS SAUCES

MEAT ON TOASTED NOODLES & MUSHROOM *DASHI*

For years your non-European Kitchenboy has been running away from passé reduced Marmite-ish sauces or thickened slurries which have been flooding most main courses in his eating experience. Small wonder then that he is so partial to simple Oriental broths and stirred-together decoctions served with meat. Then came a young local chef and radically changed his view of saucing. What subtle slyness it takes to create an entirely new fashion. Like all great inventions, one is often startled by the simplicity & obviousness of the innovation.

I met the painfully shy John Salgado when he won the 1998 Indigenous Chef of the Year Competition (professional category), which I organised for the ARC (Agricultural Research Council) to celebrate UN World Food Day. And when I recently went to review the restaurant at The Hyatt Hotel for Radio 702 with The Fairy, my regular dining companion, I was delighted to find Salgado doing time there as sous-chef. And his magic wand shone all over the fare.

The Fairy ordered a dish which stopped me in my tracks and haunted me for weeks till I tried my own version. *Grilled Veal Cutlets with Polenta in Chicken*

Broth garnished with bits of carrot & leek. On the face of it just pap & vleis, really, even if the polenta was glorified Italian pap made with milk and flavoured with fried onion, garlic, rosemary, parsley, mozzarella & Parmesan. But the clear broth was the flash notion of genius.

The most elegant broth in all the world remains the Japanese flagship *dashi*, a kind of tea extracted from dried shavings of bonito (a small species of tuna), *konbu* seaweed, and flavoured with *sake*. But such good quality instant *dashi* is now available that it really is an easy alternative to chicken stock. And noodles are born to bathe in it. I still believe noodles are at their prime when toasted a little as the Chinese do and I finally cracked the trick of keeping them together in a presentable koekie of sorts. When pre-cooking them, do not rinse afterwards – the surface starch will help them keep shape. The beauty of this broth principle is that you could use any kind of presentable grilled or braaied meat.

French cut veal, lamb, pork or game chops make for a pretty presentation when stacked like a Boy Scout fire. But rare slices of fillet of beef, venison, guinea fowl, pigeon or duck work just as well. You may think the latter is all I eat, but I have so much left over from a promotion, that my freezer quacks every time it is opened.

And see, KB *can* tart up if he has to. John Delgado, talented sous-chef at the Hyatt, introduced KB to the notion of a broth with roast meat.

BROTHS VS SAUCES

MEAT ON TOASTED NOODLES &
MUSHROOM *DASHI*

4-6 dried Chinese mushrooms
2 cups water
3 tbsp thin soy sauce (Kikkoman)
½ cup *sake* (Japanese rice wine)
2 bundles pre-cooked wheat noodles
grilled meat for 4, as per above
butter for toasting the noodles
2 tsp instant dashi stock

- Soak the mushrooms for ½ hour, cut off stems & slice thinly.
- Combine water, soy & *sake*, simmer & add mushrooms.
- Pre-cook noodles, drain, but don't rinse.
- Pile noodles into 2 small oiled bowls & invert onto oiled plate to set.
- Braai or grill the meat as you like it, rest a few minutes
& slice if using fillets.
- Unmould noodles & fry in butter till crisp on top & bottom.
- Ladle broth & mushrooms into
deep plate, place noodle cake in middle.
- Stack meat around the noodles & garnish as you please.
- Serve immediately.

This 3-meter long oil, *Flying Dutchman*, has KB & then-wife Wimpie in the foreground, but the figure in the corner started his tampering with the Old Masters, as below.

Venus with a Vibrator, a 1½ meter chalk drawing, has been exhibited in several art museums and much has been written about its sexuality. In reality the sex toy wasn't contrived to have any special meaning. When KB drew the hand, it simply reminded him of the hand in a corny 50's ad in an Afrikaans magazine, where a beehived woman held a vibrator against her neck "to relieve everyday tension." But he has always resented that these are only available in seedy venues and has taken many a bashful woman on an incognito shopping expedition

~~VINDALOO~~

DUCK VINDALOO

Your histrionic Kitchenboy rides the high seas to Goa, where Portuguese explorers introduced fiery red chillies to India, forever changing the face of their national cuisine. That is the rightfully earned fusion, a region's food moulded by its climate and its proud history, turbulent epochs of conquerors, wars, persecution and famines. Not prissy little dishes contrived and proclaimed by fashionable contemporary chefs.

The colonising Portuguese did not only bring chillies to Goa, they also introduced Christianity and thus wine & pork. The word *vindaloo* comes from their wine & garlic sauce (*vin d'alho*) and pork is still the traditional meat in the vindaloos of the Konkani-speaking Christians of the west coast of India. Vindaloo is a culinary technique rather than a dish, whereby the meat is first marinated in voluptuously flavoured vinegar, which cuts the fattiness of pork, lamb, chicken or duck (which I deem the best of all). It has the reputation of being the hottest of all curries, barely short of lifting your skull, in fact. I was introduced to duck vindaloo by the late Peter Noël-Barham in his bygone Joubert Park restaurant, The Perfumed Garden. When he casually enquired about my impressions, I couldn't squeak forth a single syllable. I was ablaze. And hooked.

A decent curry is never made with that endemic spice-dust we inherited from trite British Victorian cooking, which still renders all dishes it invades identical. No self-respecting Indian cook would ever make a curry without first making a 'wet masala' (a paste of garlic, fresh ginger and chillies), and a garam masala (carefully chosen spices first dry-toasted to release their aromatic volatile oils, and then ground finely). Ghee is the preferred oil for browning. It is

basically clarified butter. which keeps better in hot climates since it is the milk solids in butter that quickly turn rancid.
Please don't be disheartened by the seemingly elaborate preparation. it wouldn't rob you of more than 15 minutes. And you will own the key to all your subsequent curry adventures. This one can be made a day before – some cooks even insist on it. Freezes well too. old bachelor. But I like it freshly made as follows.

KB in drag (the others are real). during a party given by an actor-friend & notorious cross-dresser.

VINDALOO

DUCK VINDALOO

WET MASALA
1 big thumb fresh ginger
6 large cloves garlic
8 fresh long red chillies (adapt according to your bravado)

- Peel ginger & garlic, add chillies and process to a paste

GARAM MASALA
1 tbsp cumin
2 tbsp mustard seeds
6 cardamom pods (shelled)
10 black peppercorns
2 tsp coriander seeds
2 tsp turmeric powder
¼ tsp cloves, powdered
1 tsp cinnamon powder
chilli powder (optional for masochists)

- Toast spice seeds in a skillet or wok over a low heat till aromatic, not burnt. Pound, grind or process and add to turmeric, cloves & cinnamon.

GHEE
½ cup butter

- Melt in a small pan or microwave and strain through a tea-strainer

THE VINDALOO
1 cup wine vinegar
1 duck, portioned
salt
2 onions, sliced
1 tsp sugar

- Combine the spices and paste with the vinegar and marinate the duck for 24 hours in a non-metal container. (I seal everything in a plastic bag, all air squeezed out). • Remove the duck (saving the marinade), season with salt and fry till golden in a heavy lidded pot. • Fry the onions till they start colouring and drain off the oil (duck fat & ghee). • Add the marinade and cover tightly with the lid. • Cook very slowly till the duck is tender, about 30 minutes. • Stir in the sugar at the last minute to take the edge off the vinegar. • Serve with basmati rice & garnish with coriander leaves.

Kitchenboy as an Admiral was originally an official Naval commission. KB wanted it to have the feeling of our historical maritime art, harking back to our Portuguese heritage, hence the swarthy complex of the officer and the rather vulgarly elaborate frame. The Jules Vernesque monster and the lonely woman on a shark-encircled island is also very much part of a seaman's life. Hardly surprisingly, it was rejected. An enraged KB painted his own portrait over it

You don't need to make this much at a time, I often make only an arm's length, stuffing it with a wooden bung through a large funnel. My ex-mother-in-law, Joan Cilliers of Dwaalboom, was the Bosveld queen of Boerewors. This is her recipe. Hello Joan, how's ou Jaap? Love to Wimpie.

BOEREWORS

HOME-MADE BOEREWORS

MEAT
100 g casings, pork, large
1.5 kg beef, topside
500 g lamb, boneless leg
500 g sheep's tail fat
125 g spek (pork back fat)

FLAVOURINGS
40 ml whole coriander seeds
15 ml black pepper, ground
20 ml salt
5 ml nutmeg, freshly grated
5 ml powdered cloves
75 ml brown vinegar

- In your kitchen sink, wash the casings (a lot if salted). One at a time, pull one end over the cold tap and, holding it, rinse inside well but oppas, it's much longer than you expect and instantly turns into something between a firehose and a pofadder.
- Let the casings soak in a bowl of acidulated water (i.e. with half a lemon's juice) till needed.
- Toast coriander seeds in a dry pan until aromatic and just colouring. They burn quickly, so remove immediately and grind them in a blender or mortar & pestle. Add to all other spices.

— BOEREWORS —

- To grind the meat, you can simply ask your small butcher to mince it for you, or you can do it yourself, but only through a coarse grinding plate. Fine mince invariably indicates poor quality meat. If you're pleasurably insane, chop it with two even-weighted knives, as I did, but know this is quite a mission. (Jissem, in my kiekie-comic I'm chopping so fast you can't even see the knives.)
- Put all the meat in a large bowl, sprinkle the spices over, then the vinegar.
- With your fingers, toss everything thoroughly but *very lightly*, do not squash the meat. The secret of good boerewors lies in loosely packed meat, not densely stuffed.
- To taste and adjust the flavour, fry a tiny frikkadel of meat and try it.
- Fit the funnel on a meat grinder without cutting blade or plate, and then slip the end of a wet casing over the tip of the funnel and slide all the rest of it over too. If you don't smile secretly, you're not doing it correctly.
- Let someone feed the meat into the mouth of the grinder while you guide the growing wors with your hands. Do not overfill, keep an even thickness and prevent air pockets. Boerewors is left in continuous coils, and is not twisted into coils.
- To cook, lay it down in a large or small spiral and pierce across with skewers (see picture), to facilitate handling.
- Braai or grill on a rifflepan (cold to start with) on both sides till barely cooked, still swimming with juice inside.

Never, ever, overcook boerewors and don't prick holes in it.

DRY WORS

Omit the spek, which turns rancid. Hang in a cool, draughty place, without touching. As the meat shrinks it clings to the casing, leaving air in the centre. So squeeze flat after 2 days. Alternatively, use thin sheep runners.

Detail of a semi-nude of the wildly esoteric ex-girlfriend Isabella Smook. An ardent but innocent patron proudly displayed it to her staff. until KB pointed out the scattered semen on her chest. They were lovers during artist Braam Kruger's personality change to Kitchenboy. The sketch below was the first logo.

CHIMICHURRI SAUCE

Don't cry for Argentina's *asado*, Cowboy, cry for our Boere-braaivleis. Your losgat Kitchenboy galloped his visiting ex-wife & her new husband Jan, to a Buenos Aires-style restaurant recently and promptly requested the barbecued bull's testicles, a specialty of the grill-house. He figured it would be fitting that he & Jan symbolically shared a pair as a toast to their mutual attraction to an exceptional woman.

Too bad the macho balls were not available at such short notice. 'Order three days in advance, please,' restaurateur Vasco Velho likes to serve them *really* fresh at El Fuego. But it did have me marvelling at the unusual cuts and variety meats (as in offal) the Argentineans turn to magic on their national braai, the *asado*. It is an entirely alternative way of thinking about braaiing, which has me crying about our stodgy vleis, pap & sous by comparison.

Asado has its humble origins in the makeshift outdoor cooking of the 19th century cowboy – *El Goucho* – of the cattle-ranching grasslands (*Las Pampas*) of Argentina, a region celebrated by serious aficionados for the best beef in the world. They would pound coarse salt into the meat, wasting little of the carcass. All this would then be grilled on cast-iron bars (*parilla*) over an open fire (*El Fuego*). The tougher, often huge, cuts would require slow roasting high above the heat, stewing in the sky, one might say.

Another sneaky reason for taking my ex to this restaurant, was their sweetbreads (*molleja*) on offer, which we regularly binged on. We did this particularly in Struisbaai, where the Bredasdorp butcher sent us a regular free supply, much amused that we actually ate the stuff they all spurned. Arguably the prince of offal, sweetbreads are the growth glands from the neck of weaning calves & lambs but they are nowadays very hard to come by.

Another peculiarity, of which I have only very vague & young memories from my oupa's farm, is grilled *chinchulines*. These are small-intestines, which my ouma would clean scrupulously and plait like koeksisters. Besides kidneys (*riñon*) and blood sausages (*morcilla*), the Argentinean chorizo is a mild-tasting 50% pork-beef sausage, echoing the best flavours we have sadly lost in our own boerewors. But it was the unexpected braai cuts of beef which startled my jaded rump steak buds. Heck, I believe one specialty even calls for the skin to be left on. *Costillar à la Parilla* (thick rib) is a long fat strip of beef with rib bones, grilled high & slow over the fire. Though

certainly not for the glass-jawed gourmet, it has all the intensified flavours of the harder-working muscles. So too is the *Vacio*, or flank steak, a large boneless cut from the lower part of the ribs, but it has to be enjoyed rare to prevent its succulent texture from tightening to toughness.

As if all wasn't remarkable enough, the uniqueness of an Argentinean *asado* lies in the *chimichurri*, which accompanies all their grilled meats. It is a sublime vinegar-parsley sauce, or rather an uncooked dressing, which is well worth trying if you too are gatvol of our plebeian pap-en-sous kultuur. Simply sprinkle crushed coarse salt over meat immediately before braaiing, rest a little when cooked and sprinkle the *chimichurri* over as you eat. Mouthwatering on spit-braaied lamb and even as a marinade for chicken.

ARGENTINA

EL FUEGO'S CHIMICHURRI SAUCE (VINEGAR-PARSLEY SAUCE)

35 ml white wine vinegar

50 ml sunflower oil (I prefer olive oil)

3 tbsp Italian parsley, finely chopped

1 tsp dried origanum

1 clove garlic, finely chopped

1 tsp paprika

2 tsp chilli flakes

Mix all together and let stand for 2 to 8 hours.

Darling friendgirl Nicky Stubbs (aka Stella Nova), whose alias stems from this pose, assumed after a little wine. Stella Nova was a photographic studio known for such cheesy portraits. With her brilliant career in publishing, she has been a prime instigator of this and other books.

Kitchenboy
ON COUSCOUS

The line between good & bad taste in art, food and all other things is so flimsy, that even KB's rule of thumb doesn't always hold up; that it's okay as long as you are not a victim of it.

the sacrilege. There is only one way, and that is the palace way. And he should know, after all, he was a chef in the Moroccan palace for years. Though he steams couscous in his own restaurant, I have often caught him taking my shortcut in a rush. And there never was a contract out on my life, which I know of.

Proper traditional couscous is painstakingly made (don't worry, not by you), by an Arab sprinkling drops of water onto a thin layer of fine semolina in a tray, and then rolling tiny pellets under a patient, knowing palm. It is then steamed in stages over an aromatic vegetable broth in a couscousier. God be praised for liberated woman and precooked couscous. Moroccans never use salt, but I don't like its raw, bland taste, and prefer using hot chicken stock (common old cubes are fine).

SKELM COUSCOUS
Equal ratio water (or stock) to couscous. Pour boiling liquid over couscous in a glass bowl, two fingers above the grains, and let stand till completely absorbed. Aim at a dryish grain but remember that if not fully moisturised, it will swell unkindly in your belly. Toss terribly lightly with 2-prong fork or chopsticks till crumbly. Some add a little oil & the colonial French add butter. Cover with cling wrap (my, how this has changed the face of cooking) and microwave till the bottom of the bowl is blerrie hot to the touch. Loosen grains once more and heap high onto a tray. Don't pat it down.

Couscous is usually eaten with *tajines,* so named after the flat earthenware dish with conical lid in which they are cooked. The Moroccan version of potjiekos, I guess. But if they scorn potjiekos as contemptuously as I do, there is sure to be a contract out on my life. It is served over the couscous, topped by a bizarre but delirious spicy onion-raisin jam called *tfia* and decorated with deep-fried almonds, accompanied by their merci-less chilli sauce, *harissa*. You and your guests will delight in the exotic per-fumed aromas of cinnamon, cardamom and saffron which permeate your home during the long stewing time, and Mostapha's palace recipe will feed your entire harem.

Moroccan chef Mostapha Qotb, in the open Kitchenboy Restaurant kitchen; a din-ers' view. Formerly working for a royal palace in Morocco, this notoriously radi-cal venue & its food was a serious eye-opener for him, but he survived to start

COUSCOUS

LAMB TAJINE
SOUS COUSCOUS BEL TFIA

THE MEAT
4 kg lamb chops (leg)
3 onions, chopped
½ cup oil
1 tsp salt
big pinch saffron
1 heaped tbsp white pepper
1 heaped tbsp ginger (dry powder)
8 whole cardamom pods (bruised)
5 cinnamon sticks
water to cover
harissa sauce

• Fry the meat, onions and spices for about 10 minutes till the onions are soft. • Add water to cover the meat and slow-cook under a lid till tender. • Dish the meat into a volcano-hollow made atop the couscous heap. • Serve the cooking sauce, mixed with the *harissa* or in separate bowls.

THE TFIA
1,5 kg onions (half-rings)
1 cup water
500 g seedless raisins
salt
3 tbsp butter
1 tsp powdered ginger
1 tsp white pepper
2 high tsp cinnamon
3 strands saffron
600 g sugar

• Cook the onions in the water till soft, add the rest and cook till it attains the consistency of thin jam.

THE ALMONDS
• Boil a handful of almonds for 5 minutes, cool & peel. • Fry in oil till golden yellow (not brown, for the screaming hot oil will continue to overcook them inside when you remove them.)

Another classical send-up, this of Titian's *Man with a Blue Sleeve*, the material painted like a pink nylon parka. KB's portrait painted from memory, feigning the look all self-portraits have, as if looking in a mirror. Oil on wood panel is his preferred medium, which soaks up the paint and renders it more translucent than canvas. All his works are highly varnished too. The title & hand with Coke was added later on computer for the accompanying writing.

COCA-COLA

BRANDY & COKE MARINADE

In a prehistoric life, your hairy, arboreal Kitchenboy was so passionate about perfect fruit, that his eyes evolved to the front of his face to calculate the distance, trigonometrically, of his dive to the next laden branch. Then temperatures dropped and his lush jungle orchards disappeared forever, but the imprinting was done. And as a modern ape, he & others of his species found solace in an exotic artificial fruit from the land which gave us Superman. A most beauteous fruit called Coca-Cola.

Coca-Cola was invented by a quack named John S. Pemberton, of Atlanta, Georgia, in May 1886. His bookkeeper, Frank Robinson, came up with the name, after the main ingredients – extracts of coca leaves & cola nut. Robinson also designed the logo in Spencerian script, of what has become a representative symbol of the 20th century and its most ingenious & famous food product. Originally advertised as a headache cure, a hangover client at a local drugstore had his Coca-Cola syrup accidentally diluted with carbonated instead of still water, and the addictive soft drink was born.

More recently, a chemist friend of mine explained why he prescribed Coke for my upset tummy. Of all household ingredients, he said, including vinegar, it is the one closest in acidity to our gastric juices, and so helps to settle it down, acidity being scaled from 0 (distilled water) to 100 (gastric juices). A fruit in its ultimate state of ripeness has developed enough sugar to perfectly balance its acidity to create a natural sweet & sour pulp. Likewise, the amount of sugar in Coca-Cola syrup is almost imperceptibly neutralised by equally scary levels of phosphoric acid. And the addition of carbonated

water, I believe, simulates ferment-
ing fruit, which, as Van Riebeeck
laconically commented about
dagga, '... causes the mind to
wander.'
Coca-Cola thus being considered
by **Kitchenboy** as the ultimate
man-made fruit, and super-aesthet-
ically packaged in that gorgeous
little tart of a feminine bottle, it
begs to be used as a marinade.
Please pardon his East Rand gom-
gat streak, which could not resist
adding some brandy. Naartjie peel
is included for the love of rugby

and of being South African.

If you are short of time, strain
the marinade, boil fast in a
saucepan to reduce to a thin
syrup, amber-coating a spoon, but
do not let it darken. Then paint it
onto the meat before & during the
braai. Very *teriyaki*. As a glaze or
as a marinade, use it with beef,
game, fish, shellfish (calamari!),
pork, poultry (especially skinless
chicken thighs) to braai, grill or
roast. Or use it as a cook-in sauce
braising the meat till tender and
the marinade thickened.

KB's well-lubricated bachelor days, with friendgirls, actors Marguerite,
Nicole & Bianca, at a glorious downtown dive serving only Congolese
fare, Kin Malebo.

~~COCA-COLA~~

BRANDY & COKE MARINADE

3 cups Coca-Cola
1 cup good, light soy sauce
juice of 2 limes or 1 lemon
¼ cup brandy
1 medium onion, sliced
1 naartjie's peel, sliced in strips
6 cloves garlic, peeled
3 or more fresh chillies, chopped
1 stick cinnamon
1 star anise
2 tbsp oil

- Mix the liquids together.
- Fry the solids in oil till the onions colour
(or else they'll go sour).
- Drain & blot off oil.
- Chuck solids into liquid & muck around a bit.
It gets better every day as the flavours infuse in your fridge.
I swear by plastic bags. Just gooi meat & marinade into a bag,
press all air out and make a knot at the liquid-level.
This reduces the risk of contamination.
- Marinate for a day or so.
- Paint a little oil on the meat & braai,
while you reduce the marinade to a sauce.

Kitchenboy

The boar's head as a symbol of a feast is an ancient one. But KB's version originated from his drunken art student days, drawing the boar's head logo from the Gordon's Vodka label. (see page 94). Inevitably, it became the head of a warthog. The background scenery has his

~~CRACKLING~~

TWICE-COOKED BELLY OF PORK

The thought that he might hurt or offend the spiritual dedication of his Jewish & Muslim friends, makes your gastronomically agnostic Kitchenboy cringe in embarrassment. Yet that unclean & forbidden animal in so many societies, the pig, is so important in Christian and Far Eastern cultures, that it cannot be excluded from a culinary point of view. So askies & sorry, but here follows some glory to the fat vark.

Where there is smoke there is fire, for many ancient health guides parade as religious laws, as in pork. Trichinosis, a parasitical disease contaminating fresh & cured pork, which can be transferred to humans, may now be minimised by healthy farming practices, but it is still very real. To avoid this health hazard, it is generally recommended that pork be cooked to medium-doneness (internal temperature of 66°C/150°F).

However, this paranoia usually leads to the overcooking and poor culinary reputation of pork. Relax. Just poke a skewer into the thickest part and eye the colour of the pressurised cooking juice oozing out of the gaatjie (the heat has driven all the moisture to the centre). If it is pink, prolong the cooking, if it is clear it is perfect, and if no juice comes forth you have ruined it, finish en klaar.

Its flesh is curiously pale in colour, like chicken, because its notoriously lazy nature demands a minimum of red oxygen-storing myoglobin in its muscles. But also, of all meats we know, pork and especially its undomesticated relatives like the warthog & wild boar, is by far the driest, because the fat is stored in one layer under the skin and not marbled into the meat as in beef. The belly & deboned neck are two exceptions and deservedly favourite cuts among the Chinese. Transforming the skin into crisp, bubbly crackling is one of the prime joys of oven-roasting pork, even if I tend to resist such élitist wasting of energy, which is why I recently chose to first steam this belly of pork (to render it safe) and to finish it on the braai. This recipe also proves my suspicion that the skin turns leathery in wet heat (steaming) and into crackling when exposed to dry heat (roasting & braaiing). Rubbing fine salt into the scored skin further draws out moisture from the skin to assist its crunchy transformation.

Drop-dead gorgeous & cherished friendgirl, talented actor Bianca Amato, currently a famous soap-star, whose fine intellect and suss will pave her way to the skies.

CRACKLING

TWICE-COOKED BELLY OF PORK

1 kg belly of pork (deboned)
water for steaming
2 tsp fine salt
3 tbsp soy sauce
1 tbsp hoisin sauce
1 tbsp brown sugar
1 tsp minced fresh ginger

- Score thin parallel cuts into the skin with a razor-sharp knife.
I used a Stanley knife, but for God's sake be careful,
I damn nearly lost my boyhood when it slipped!
- Steam for about an hour or till cooked when tested.
- Dry thoroughly and rub the salt into the scored skin.
- Melt the rest of the ingredients together and paint onto the
exposed meat (not the skin).
- Grill slowly over a braai till the crackling is crisp and
the sauce caramelised.
(By the way, any other barbecue sauce like *teriyaki* can be used
instead of the delicious concoction above).
- Serve hot or at room temperature.

ALTERNATIVE
If you want to oven-roast it instead, skip the steaming and
roast it on a rack at 180 °C/350 °F for about an hour or
till cooked when tested.

Fair Game

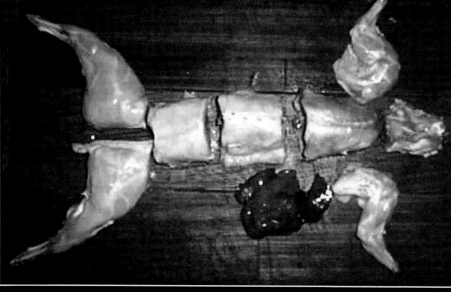

Hunting wild rabbits with his mongrel greyhound on his way to the river was a exhilarating part of fishing for the young KB. But once, to alert the dog to a fleeing har he tapped her on the gat with the point of his fishing rod, which accidentally lodged th hook firmly into her skin. It was an unforgettable chase: dog jaaging rabbit & boy jaagin dog with a screeching reel.

crisp potato croquettes on the side. Wild rabbits & hares belong to the same family, *Leiporidae*, the latter larger with longer ears, longer hind legs and darker, gamier flesh, but both make for excellent eating. I old *New Larousse Gastronomique* supplies us with a diagram to distinguish between the bones of their respective forelegs. Bit late, I'd say.

But it is the farmed or hatch rabbit on which we focus here, because

their availability. Notoriously difficult to farm, rabbit supplies are
often irregular; try Italian &
Portuguese butchers. Though all rabbits are traditionally designated to
stewed & braised dishes, to which
they take admirably, their mild

flavour is better appreciated when
pan-fried or grilled on a riffle-plate.
Lean & very pale, rabbit should be
classified as white meat. The flavour
is akin to chicken and the texture
firm like loin of pork, making timing
of the utmost importance.

SAVING THE WORLD FROM BAD TASTE is a commercial slogan of KB, really referring to his play
on values in art, particularly what is considered good or bad art, as seen in the two backgrounds
of this *Portrait of Picasso as Olympia*. You choose.

RABBIT

PREPARING & PAN-FRYING RABBIT

Rabbits are sold with the coveted liver still in place. An endearing custom is to serve this as a starter to the guest of honour. Jointing a rabbit is as easy as chicken, though you'll need a sturdy knife to cut through the backbone. The ribs & flanks (cut in strips) can be fried crisply as garnish.

All rabbits benefit from barding or larding with bacon (try slivers of chorizo sausage inserted in little cuts), but this is not necessary if you ensure its juiciness by staying with it while cooking. The imperative test for doneness is the moment clear juices ooze out from the hole where straw or skewer pierced the thick part of a joint. Season the cutlets, pan-fry in butter with a tad of garlic & simply deglaze the pan with a splash of fruit juice, port or wine. Or serve with this rather offbeat but simple sweet-sour berry sauce I concocted for your pleasure. Good for pan-fried rabbit, chicken, pork, game or deep-fried fish.

RASPBERRY & CAMPARI SAUCE

2 cups pink grapefruit or orange juice
2 tbsp strawberry jam
1 thumb fresh ginger, bruised
2 sticks cinnamon
2 large red chillies, chopped
½ cup red wine vinegar
2 tots Campari
½ cup sugar
½ tsp salt
2 X 125 g punnets raspberries

- Boil up everything except 1 punnet raspberries,
  till well infused & a bit syrupy.
- Remove saucepan from heat.
- Discard cinnamon & ginger and chuck in the rest of the berries.
- Serve with crisp potato croquettes, shoestring chips or grilled polenta

Kitchenboy
ON
Steak Tartare

KB's obsession with equestrian drawings had a rather plebeian origin. When demonstrating his prowess as an artist, his schoolchums insisted that he draws a rearing horse (the only image they could relate to art), but he could never quite crack the complex hooves of horses, until he read that it was really just a big toenail, and everything fell into place.

STEAK TARTARE

ORIENTAL STEAK TARTARE ON THE PLATE

In a fierce but former lifetime, your marauding Tartar Kitchenboy was galloping over the Asian Steppes with his meat ration pounding underneath him, between horse and saddle, to tenderise and cure. Some aficionados to this day maintain that the authentic dish that bears these tribesmen's name, Steak Tartare, is made from horse, rather than beef.

My first encounter was not a happy one. Even as a near-starving artist at an exhibition opening in Antwerp, where I usually went for supper, I was so horrified to discover that the topping of my finger food was raw mince, that I promptly hid it behind a pot plant. Yet I grew addicted to it, as street food in this city, simply spread on an open roll and pressed into chopped onion.

But minced meat from a butchery it most certainly is not. Tellingly, the Flemish still call mince *gehackt* (literally, hacked). Queen Victoria banned the new hand-cranked mincing gadgets from the palace, because she rightly claimed it squeezes all the juice from the meat, as the Orientals too believe. The only way to correctly prepare meat for tartare, is to hack it with two even-weighted or -sized knives, with limp wrists and a rhythmic drumbeat. And only the best quality, fat-free and gristle-free meat will do, invariably fillet. It has become fashionable to make tartare with game & fish like tuna or salmon, but traditionally, and still the best, is beef.

And traditionally it is not the fanfare made of it in restaurants. Even Paul Bocuse cites only raw egg yolk on top, capers, chopped onion & parsley. But I have feasted on a bewildering range of tartare, mixed at your table in posh or pretentious establishments or by yourself, with all ingredients prettily arranged around the meat, to try morsels of different flavour combinations. Much to my resentment, it is often mixed in the kitchen, arriving at your table like a formidable raw hamburger patty. Their ingredients include chopped gherkins, capers, olives, onions, parsley & other herbs, lemon juice, Worcester & Tabasco sauce, cognac, paprika, salt & pepper. Like *sashimi* (and condensed milk, for that matter), one can't have too much of it, and a 100 g portion is more than ample, as an elegant starter.

That is exactly what I offered last weekend to my food-loving friends Claire, Bianca & Big John, who is forever trying to outdo me gastronomically. But I figured since there aren't any real rules, why not return to its supposed Asian origins, and play with the blistering array of Oriental flavours which are becoming increasingly available in this country. The gang raved, as will you

Another Steak Tartare evening in KB's yellow dining room, with Nicole, Claire & Junglegirl.

STEAK TARTARE

ORIENTAL
STEAK TARTARE

ON THE PLATE
100 g beef fillet per person
fresh quail eggs
spring onion, minced
dhania, chopped
basil or mint, chopped
radish (daikon or red), shredded
dried shrimp, finely chopped
pickled mustard greens, chopped
wasabi, prepared
lemon wedges

ON THE TABLE
soy sauce
oyster sauce
chilli sauce
sesame oil
pepper oil (aka chilli oil)
Thai fish sauce (*nam pla*)
sake (Japanese rice wine)
5-spice powder
salt

• Cut the fillet in small squares. • With two knives, chop the meat, using a criss-cross movement, till fairly fine but not pasty (see small pic on page 146). Do not overhandle the meat; loosen with a fork and form a flattened ball. • Place in middle of the plate. • Top the quail's eggs and separate. • Put the yolk back into the shell and stand on top of the meat. • With a teaspoon, arrange little heaps of the solid ingredients in a circle around the meat and serve, passing around the condiments. You could have Melba toast with it but that spoils the exotic feel of it all. • Serve with *sake* on the rocks.

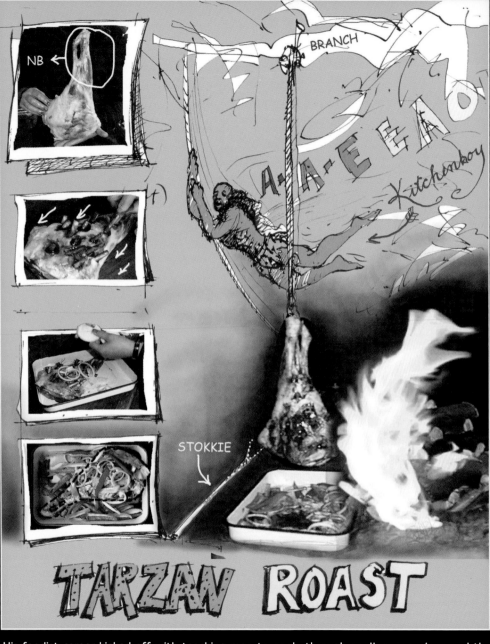

TARZAN ROAST

His foodist career kicked off with teaching men to cook, through angling magazines and the likes of *Playboy SA*. That forever tainted KB's writing style, concentrating on and figuring out the mechanics of how food behaves in fire, even if just an educated guess, rather than offering lifeless recipes.

~~TARZAN ROAST~~

THE TARZAN ROAST

A-A-A-A-A-A-A-I-I-I-I-I-E-E-E-A-A-A-A-A-A-A-I-I-I-E-E-E-A-A-A-A-A-A-!-!-!-! The jungle foliage bursts open and your windgat Kitchenboy swings through the parting on a wild vine-rope, hollering that spine-chilling victory cry, made famous by his many biographers and emulators. But bioscope this is not, for he has just reinvented an ancient French roasting technique for your impending braaivleis pleasure.

To poise yourself for my Tarzan Roast, think of it as a vertical spit, not unlike a rotating shwarma-grill.

Now imagine suspending a large roast on a rope from an overhanging branch next to a raging fire, NOT above. Sorry to gaan aan like this about the positioning of the meat, but to my horror, whenever my recreation went into the public domain, it was perverted into something very different by hanging it right above the coals. This would simply dry out the meat, change the taste with flare-ups and in all probability, burn the rope & drop the roast onto the fire. Jaaaaaa.

Properly cooked in the radiated heat (reflection or glare of the fire), you will impart a scrumptious subtlety to the meat, unattainable by other roasting techniques. The cooking times are somewhat longer (we're talking suspended stewing times, really), and because the fat falls into a drip tray, and not on the fire, it is spared the acrid bitterness of flaring fat. Instead it is enchanted by gentler hardwood smoke, which sporadically enfolds it. You will also continually baste it with the drippings in the tray underneath, sweetened as the sugar-rich veggies and flavourings slow-roast in the glare. You will lovingly tend the meat, continually touching it (feeling if it gets hot enough), occasionally rotating it to face the fire (that's what the sharpened stokkie in the picture is for) and inhale the developing aromas. Thus it is an infinitely more aesthetic experience, which distinguishes your feeding from a beast's, rather than slamming it into a Defy.

Leg of lamb is brilliantly suited, but so is game (i.e. impala) and kid (from a young Karoo boerbok). Whatever leg you choose, the fattier the better, it is imperative that the shank bone remains uncut (see step 1 on page 150). Flavouring too, is arbitrary (a simple oil-rub and seasoning will do marvellously), though my guinea-friends pronounced this rather tongue-in-cheek recipe superlative. Feel free to cook the Tarzan Roast in your kitchen hearth or an oven @ 200 °C. The stokkie doubles as your Flintstones meat thermometer. Zap it into the thickest part and check the colour of the oozing juice: bright red is raw, bright pink is rare, pink is medium-rare and no juice means you feed it to the dogs.

Be sure the meat hangs really close to the heat, where your hand can't stand it longer than a few seconds. A disgruntled fan once cornered me in a pub in a remote dorpie in the Karoo, and said: 'Ek is altyd gaar voor die vleis.' (I'm invariably pissed before the meat is cooked.) Easy on the dop & tune up the fire, Swaer.

A tray of beautiful sweets has always been a trademark of KB's restaurant & house foyers, as well as a pretty vase with tampons & condoms in his bathroom.

TARZAN ROAST

THE TARZAN ROAST

1 leg of lamb (fatty, shank intact)
8 cloves garlic, slivered
a few red chillies, whole
2 bunches spring onions (sturdy light part only)
½ cup oyster sauce
1 big onion, in rings
2 bell peppers, red & yellow, strips
¼ cup balsamic vinegar
½ cup olive oil

- At a sharp angle (towards upper leg), sink shafts into the meat by cutting an X with a small blade and opening the hole with a finger.
- Insert a sliver of garlic in each and some small chillies here and there.
- Dip a spring onion into oyster sauce and then force it into the whole.
- Continue till it looks like St Sebastian on your table.
- Lay it in a shallow tray, cover with rest of ingredients, and let it marinate till you are ready to roast and baste it as explained before.
- Rest it in a warm place for at least 10 minutes before carving.
- Cup your hands before your mouth and yodel into the night.

Commissioned by a filmmaking couple, this painting of the netherworld again features a pony-tailed self-portrait, the *Tree of Life* (bearing breast-fruit) and God with a gun.

~~KANGAROO~~

BILTONG-CARPACCIO

Damn fearless, your undaunted Kitchenboy, wouldn't you say? Who else would dare to prepare 25 kg of game he has never seen, touched, tasted or cooked before, for 49 equally virgin but game guests at his recent birthday party. Kangaroo, nogal. Truth is, once you understand the basic nature of meat and the universal qualities of the different cuts, you could tackle a Patagonian Mountain Dog if pressed to do so.

Looking blind at any meat, you can tell what kind of flesh you're dealing with. Unlike docile domesticated mammals and fowl, wild kangaroo, like most game, has dark red meat. This is not due to more blood, as I often hear, but indicates that the high work rate of the muscles requires lots of oxygen, stored in myoglobin in the cells of the muscles. Wild animals (i.e. outside zoos) have little fat, a mere 2% in kangaroo. Therefore it is imperative that any dry-cooking (as in braaiing, grilling, frying & roasting) of the tender cuts (fillet, rump, steaks), has to be done rare. Once the moisture has left the meat, it will be quite inedible to any but the most primitive palates.

I had a veritable jol! Fibrous pieces need long, slow cooking to break it down to gelatin, so I made a rather classical Kangaroo Soup with Tofu and a delicious braised affair with onions, prunes, apples, 2 bottles of Old Brown Sherry and a moerse lot of cinnamon. Finer cuts were transformed to elaborate but rare stir-fries, kebabs and roasts on the fire with passionate sauces and bastes.

But the scene-stealer was my Kangaroo Biltong-Carpaccio starter. I hit on the idea (blush), because the 3 days before the party wasn't enough to cure the biltong, so I

KANGAROO

used balsamic vinegar instead of the ominous brown vinegar we Boere traditionally use. Besides, paper-thin slices of meat 'cook' almost instantly in acidic dressings with vinegar or lemon juice and so the lovely natural red turns to a very dead gray. Neither do I use sugar, for I find game sweeter than beef already. Any game can be used (even ostrich & wild duck), but the cuts are seriously important. Strips of fillet, rump or other muscle from the hind leg, cut with the grain where possible, and all gristle, fleece and tendons removed.

KB was delighted to find this old pin-up of May Britt in a junk shop. It hung in the restaurant as his 1st wanking-picture, which sparked his kinky bent on cheesecake art, stiletto heels and platinum blondes.

KANGAROO

KANGAROO (OR GAME) BILTONG-CARPACCIO

1 kg kangaroo or other game
½ cup coriander seed
3 cloves
6 allspice, whole
4 tsp black pepper, whole
1½ cups coarse salt
balsamic vinegar
extra-virgin olive oil
crushed black pepper
capers (optional)

• Do not wash the meat, but dry it thoroughly. • Toast the coriander in a dry pan over a low heat till aromatic but not brown. Crush it coarsely. • Grind the cloves, allspice & pepper finely in a blender or old coffee-grinder. • Mix all the spices with the salt.
• Moisten (don't soak) the meat with the vinegar and place it in layers in a glass or plastic container, sprinkling each layer evenly with the cure mixture. • Cover with cling wrap & stand overnight in the fridge (about 12 hours, longer if the pieces are thick).
• Shake off the grains of salt, dry thoroughly and hang up by wire hooks or string in a draughty, dry place, away from pets, pests & sun.
• Leave for 2 to 3 days (or 7+ days for proper biltong). • With a razor-sharp knife held at a deep angle (\\\\\) slice in large paper-thin slivers and arrange on a platter. • Dribble with extra-virgin olive oil and scatter plenty of black pepper over, dotted with capers.
• Stand for 30 minutes before serving.

Portrait of KB as an Artist, with exotic vegetables, after Archimboldo. He has an obsession for rare & new produce (after all those overcooked boereboontjies of his youth),
and often tries to inspire farmers to plant them, with little success.

~~VEGETABLES~~

THE SECRET OF BRIGHT GREEN VEGETABLES

Looking down his gnarled and tuberous nose at those miserably overcooked vegetables, as calmly served to him and his guests at a pretentiously fashionable establishment, your gatvol Kitchenboy wondered how we let restaurants get away with such culinary indifference. A local phenomenon he haughtily refers to as Hotel School Vegetables (of the three-veg kind), is where he believes the rot set in. Of all things we cook, plant foods are the most vulnerable and fragile of ingredients we force onto fire.

The issue here is to understand that wondrous bright green colour only the Orientals always achieve. It is caused by the sudden expansion and escape of gases trapped in the spaces beneath the cells, which makes the pigment (in this case green chlorophyll) more directly visible. One of the biggest threats to the colour chlorophyll is acid. Indeed, that gross old-fashioned custom of adding baking soda does make the water alkaline and the veggies greener, but it also has negative side effects. A far sounder practice is to use copious amounts of water to dilute the natural acids leaking from the plant's damaged cell structure, which is caused by prolonged heating. Any technique of overcooking will bring the vegetable's acid in contact with its chlorophyll, resulting in those sickly grey-green beans, the way my ouma used to make them.

But this won't happen if you cook them in a flash, as the Chinese do. Ever seen Chinese salad? Of course not. I once read they dare not eat it raw because they use night soil as fertiliser, and to render it safe to eat they have to blanch it, a technique they have perfected. For your eternal enlightenment, I took two identical bundles of Oriental water spinach (aka *ong choi*) to two neighbouring chop shops in my beloved New Chinatown in Cyrildene and asked them to prepare it while I watched intently. Of course I could have chosen any of the baffling & marvellous range of Chinese greens sold on the strip, and you may use

VEGETABLES

any other frail green vegetables like spinach (and their stems), *maro-go*, watercress, lettuce, broccoli, young pumpkin shoots & leaves, endive, red cabbage, beet tops, white cabbage (yuk), radicchio, rocket, dandelion, nettle, asparagus, celery, green beans & snow peas.

THE SECRET OF BRIGHT GREEN VEGETABLES

CHEF 1
The first chef threw them into a huge wok of boiling water. Dunked for ten, maybe fifteen seconds, I tell you. No longer. Then fished them out with a strainer. Then he did something which absolutely stunned me into silence. He poured blerrie chicken fat over it, for God's sake. I always wondered why mine never tasted quite the same.

CHEF 2
This went so fast I will have to relate it TV-style. Clangelang! Wok onto the fiery gas-flame. Glob-glob-glob.... a little oil into

The lilo parties @ KB HQ are notorious for the behaviour of the otherwise fairly decent revellers. Among the zoo of inflatables, a male blow-up doll floated keel-down and motionless, to the horror of KB's business visitors. During a serious meeting in his studio, a friendgirl walked through while undressing and duly dived into the pool. Nobody said a word.

VEGETABLES

wok. Splat! Lots of chopped garlic to flavour the oil. Swoosh! All the greens at once (notice how they're cut into equal lengths). Shovel-shovel… uh, uh, uh, fast and furious with the spatula and immediately, dash-dash, two or three shots oyster sauce. (Oh never mind, we didn't see that whiff of flying MSG.) And another churn or two till the barely wilted vegetables are scooped onto a platter, twenty seconds later. Aaaah, shining, bright and green. These two examples apply equally to steaming, microwaving, deep-frying, grilling (on a griddle plate) or even braaiing on an open flame. Why, my darling Junglegirl, barely a few weeks ago in my kitchen, perfected young asparagus by merely pouring boiling water over them and retrieving them the precise moment they are heated through. Cooking, like making love, is not only about technique. It is also about timing, passion and understanding. You don't have to be a vegetable to think like one.

Charming, charged & complex actor friend Nick Boraine, brilliant in *Shopping & Fucking, Popcorn & Birdy*, is probably our brightest star. In KB's library

Kitchenboy on FRESH CHILLIES

Painted for KB's commercial Black Bean-Chilli Sauce. The back label goes: "bla bla bla... which she stroked & she stroked, ritualistically, until she burst into flames." His entire range was banned from a major hypermarket chain because of the naked artwork & saucy copy on their labels.

FRESH CHILLI SAUCE

Your blazing Kitchenboy is completely mystified by the blerrie **Engelse**, contradicting the most volcanic vegetable on earth by naming it a chilli. Similarly, the English-speaking world celebrates it mostly for its firepower and not its elusive taste, which is what Kitchenboy pursues in this here little hymn to the fresh chilli.

The rampant heat comes from capsaicin or, if you have to know, 8-methyl-N-vannilyn-6-nemeamide, a volatile oil which is particularly concentrated (X 20) in the white placental tissue inside the chilli. Fresh or raw chillies taste very different from cooked, pickled or dried chilli, and to fully appreciate the culinary uses of raw chilli, we have to investigate the ingredients that most enthusiastically marry with it:

ALCOHOL: Capsaicin, being a volatile oil and thus insoluble in water, infuses most willingly in alcohol. I once thoughtlessly chucked a handful of dried piri-piri chillies into a bottle of Stolichnaya (a Roald Dahl trick), and a month later, a thimble-full shooter nearly killed a stupid friend of mine. Steeping chillies in a little neat brandy, whisky or tequila for a few days, will most certainly result in a paste to test the frontiers of your madness. So take it easy, Breker.

OIL: Oil begets oil, which is why most recipes require you to fry it a little to release its flavour. Notice too how cook & guests start coughing and crying as the volatile capsaicin fumes fill the kitchen. And that is exactly how those furious chilli oils of the East are infused, by heating with sesame oil. Pound or process some fresh red chillies to a paste with olive oil and a little salt and you will have a condiment with a long fridge life.

FRESH CHILLIES

ACID: Acid also breaks down chilli and is most often used in casual dips and commercial sauces (i.e. Tabasco), doubling as a preservative. The most neutral is spirit vinegar, but vinegars made from rice, apple (cider) and wine are not as strong and have more flavour. Lime juice or lemon tastes more natural and so does tamarind.

SUGAR: This is usually included to balance the ever-present acid. The true art of dip chemistry is to dissolve the right type of sugar in a matching acid, and balance it till neither dominates. The most stupendous of my career was a coconut vinegar-palm sugar duet. So there. Palm sugar, golden brown sugar, white sugar (granulated or caster), golden syrup, honey, jams and even artificial sugar (yeah) are all suitable sweeteners. Of course the sweetness literally sugar-coats the pain. The Thais are particularly fond of blisteringly sweet chilli sauces, and so is your pleasure-seeking **Kitchenboy**.

SALT: Simply pounding fresh chilli with some coarse sea salt makes a fabulous table condiment, wherein lies the real chilli taste. In the Orient soy sauce or bean paste is often paired with the heat. And so are salty sauces or compounds with fishy overtones as in *nam pla* (Thai fish sauce), *belacan* (shrimp paste) or indeed, salted dried prawns themselves.

Outrageous & stunning Charlotte Marishani, waitron at the restaurant & later KB's assistant, pranged the Kitchmobile a week after she was named Crash.

FRESH CHILLIES

BASIC FRESH CHILLI SAUCE

4 tbsp lime or lemon juice or vinegar
4 tsp brown or palm sugar
1 tsp *nam pla* or salt
6 very hot fresh chillies, red or green (sliced)
2 tsp chopped mint
(and/or mint, ginger, garlic, dhania or spring onion)

- Mix lime or lemon juice or vinegar, sugar, *nam pla*.
- Add chilli and one, some or all of the rest.
- Use as a dipping sauce with anything fried or grilled.
Or as a wet one over fresh vegetables, fruit, sambals & salsas.

My final contribution is to suggest a supreme chilli fire-fighter, the Frozen Margarita, for it contains five of the known antidotes: alcohol (tequila), sugar (Cointreau), acid (lemon/lime juice), salt (encrusted on the glass rim) and ice.

KB & Slowmo in St Lucia, shooting the pilot for *The Kitchenboy Roadshow*. For the director's cut see page 221.

CHAKALAKA

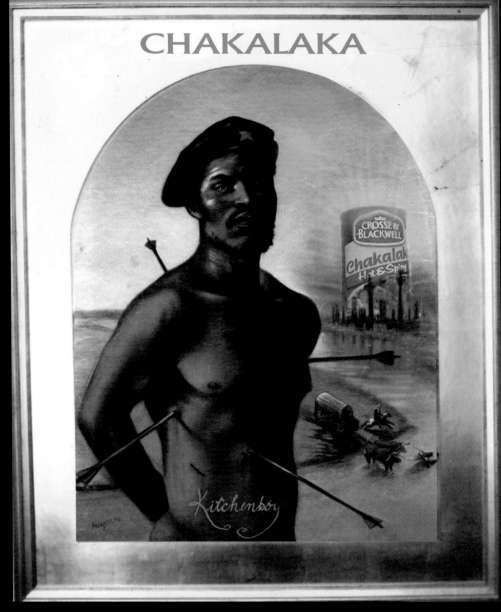

Dan Mugabe as St Sebastian, a Renaissance genre often painted by KB, tickled by the serene martyr who always seems to enjoy the pain. He never explains the meaning of his art, but associates it with events at the time of execution. Dan was his gardener, and despite his classical torso, his legs were withered away. He resented the arrows KB added to his portrait. A week or so later he seriously maimed his girlfriend with a knife.

~~CHAKALAKA~~

CHAKALAKA DU
(HOT SALAD PHEW!)

When your patriotic Kitchenboy first caught wind of a new national dish rising from the ashes of our past, he dived into the humble kitchens of his people, and triumphantly produced a fistful of scrappy notes with a proud variation offered by every person he interviewed. From the shebeens of Soweto to the super-market queues of Hillbrow and the backwaters of rural Cullinan, each amateur cook has his or her own cherished recipe.

To my shame, my first introduction to Chakalaka was the blikkies version, with a ringtop, nogal, which descended like a fever out of the townships onto our supermarket shelves from different manufacturers. I instantly fell in love with its fiery achar-esque perkiness and its versatility in giving meaning to a frugal helping of pap, rice, mash or anything charred on a braai or from the rustic stew-pots of our mini-bus taxi ranks. But over-whelmingly, I felt the exhilaration of witnessing the birth of a national condiment, to take its place along-side *seshebo*, Mrs Ball's peach chut-ney and piri-piri sauce.

I met the colourful Wandie Ndala on one of those unfortunate TV talk things, and when I discovered he was the owner of the famous Wandie's Place in Soweto, I pep-pered him with questions about Chakalaka. According to him it was developed in the stokvels and later perfected in the shebeens; but it should really be called Chakalaka du (as was confirmed elsewhere). It means Hot Salad, and the du-bit, he later explained with hilarious whistling intonations over the phone, meant 'phew!' (as in 'Shit, it's hot!'). Clearly, it is an absolute prerequisite that it lifts your skull with every morsel, thus extending & bolstering a modest meal. But it also has another hidden agenda.

Wandie claims it has to be this ferocious to cure your babbelas, for it is traditionally served with a morning braaivleis, you know, to feed that ravenous monster inside you. I have often heard that black men never eat *imifino/morogo* (cooked greens) unless seriously hung-over, and so I prodded him about it. 'It's trueee!' he crooned. A cultural variation on real men don't eat quiche? He then gave me two recipes. The first was a nowhere tomato-onion-chilli salad with tinned chilli baked beans – an abominable inclusion I encountered several times. The second sounded more feasible, and I duly concocted it. But I should have known better than to phone you just after Sunday lunch, having barely recovered from your brunch-braai, Mr Ndala, because that version would first kill the kitchenboy and then the hangover.

The following is an adaptation of Wandie's recipe, still hot as hell (or *du*), but with crunchy traditionally grated carrots, which he omits. He also leaves out the sulphurous cabbage, thank God, which most others include. Of course one can make a larney version with smartly cut vegetables, barely cooked, but this authentic one makes it truly soul food.

My understandably gourmet housekeeper, Lillian Ditse, whose enviable constitution has me whistling in the mornings, and her partying comrades declared this one superior to any Chakalaka du they've known. Just as well I caught them right after Sunday lunch, firing on all pistons again after their fortifying meal.

Charming & darling friendgirl Claudia Capelouto of Cape Town.

CHAKALAKA

CHAKALAKA DU

1 cup oil

2 heaped tbsp fresh ginger, chopped

2 heaped tbsp garlic, chopped

6 green chillies, chopped

1 large onion, coarsely chopped

50 g hot curry powder

4 tomatoes, coarsely chopped

1 green pepper, coarsely chopped

1 medium carrot, peeled & grated

1 level tsp salt

• Fry the ginger, garlic, chilli & onion a little to develop flavour.
• Add the curry powder & fry a bit to eliminate its raw floury taste.
• Add tomatoes till they release their juice. • Add the green pepper,
carrot & salt. • Switch off the stove and let it cool.
It is even better the next day.

Note: I know it seems like a *moer*-of-a-lot of oil, and you're welcome to
halve it, but this is very much the real thing. And I have seen this recipe
sneaked onto more than one upmarket restaurant menu.

Shortly after Junglegirl entered the life of restaurant
reviewer KB, she said: "Look, this week you've taken me
to a Thai restaurant, 2 Vietnamese restaurants and for
brunch we had sushi. Tonight I want KFC."

Both these details are from *St George & the Dragon*, KB's last exhibition, at the Goodman Gallery. Not without reason did he become wildly infatuated with the mesmerising & androgynous model, Natasha, who posed for all the works. It radically altered the course of his life See page 182.

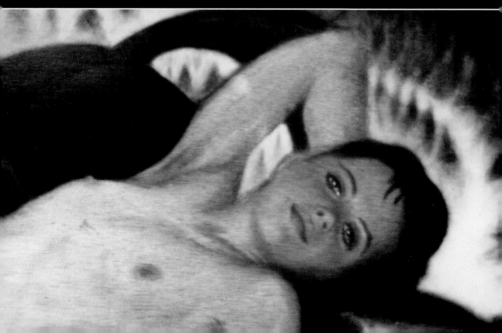

~~MEALIEPAP~~

SOFT, WET, PUTU & CRUMBLY

How clearly your 9-year-old plaasjapie Kitchenboy remembers those hectic rides from Tonteldoos to Dullstroom with his oupa Abraham in his dilapidated black 19-voertsek pickup, skidding around the narrow dust road bends on the spare wheel only. His namesake oupa, a proud man of modest means, would frequently take a few sacks of mielies, to be converted on the spot into coarse meal in the impressive cornflour-covered hammermill. That freshly ground mealie meal, and the gorgeous soft breakfast porridge slowly stewed from it, served with fresh milk & plaasbotter, would set his high standards and esteem for real mealiepap for the rest of his life.

Mealies came to our original coastal inhabitants by courtesy of the exploring Portuguese, where we get the name, from *milho*, and were passed on to the white settlers on the Eastern borders. Now you understand why you can never excite a visiting Western Kapenaar with the stodgy white stuff at your braais. Sadly, the new staple of Africa was and is also responsible for the terrible child mortality through kwashiorkor or pellagra, because unlike samp (stampmealies), mealie meal in pap form traps some of its essential nutrients.

I honestly don't believe in recipes or quantities when making mieliepap in any of its forms, because it is based primarily on intuition, principle & technique, whether made in a small stove-top pot or a huge 3-legged cast-iron potjie on an open fire. Either way, a tight-fitting lid is absolutely essential, to allow the grains to steam & swell completely, and to prevent a skin forming on top.

MEALIEPAP

HOW TO MAKE PLAIN PAP

The following basic recipes use 1 litre water & 1 tsp salt:

SOFT PORRIDGE (AKA SLAPPAP)

• Salt & remove the boiling water from the heat. • In one continuous thin stream of meal (about ¾ cup), pour it into the edge of the swirling water, return to a very low heat and keep stirring with a table fork till it splutters like boiling mud. Immediately cover tightly with a lid for about 15 minutes. Please take care, especially when you are kaalgat as the flying pap can leave nasty burns on your person and some uncomfortable explaining to do.
• Serve with a nugget of unsalted butter, fresh milk or cream
& sugar, honey or syrup.

WET PORRIDGE OR POLENTA

• Salt & remove boiling water from heat. • Stirring with a table fork, rain a continuous stream of meal (1 cup) or till it starts to thicken & cover tightly.
• Cook 45 min, stirring from time to time. • Serve as is with a topping or pour into a mould or onto a board to cool & set. Then cut in slices & pan-fry, deep-fry or paint with olive oil & grill on a riffle pan or braai fire.

Multitalented friend & actor Gideon Emery harbours an amusing wannabe-sleaze streak, for he is quite the opposite. Here with a real Hawaiian shirt from KB.

MEALIEPAP

PUTU (AKA STYWEPAP)

• Using a wooden paddle, add the meal (2 cups) as above and stir on the heat until it stiffens, turn heat to low & keep stirring vigorously until all lumpiness is squashed out against the side of the pot.

• Cover to steam for 45 minutes.

• Serve with braaivleis & sauce.

CRUMBLY PORRIDGE (AKA KRUMMELTJIEPAP)

• Into the boiling water, gooi all the meal (4 cups) in a heap in the middle. Slam the lid on very tightly, leaving the grains to swell for about 10 minutes.

• With a 2-pronged fork, very lightly work the dry meal from the middle to the wet moat around it. • Aim at keeping it crumbly or at the most very large lumps, while ensuring that no dry meal is left. Never press it into balls or solids.

• Turn the heat low and cover again to steam another 45 minutes or even 2 hours. Delicious with butter stirred in and cold milk & sugar.

Virtual dinner. When Junglegirl returned to St Lucia to settle her affairs, KB was in agony. So he dated her for dinner. Via the internet, he sent 20 red roses to both of them, they bought the same wine and food, each set a table for two. He phoned at midnight and dined intimately with his sweetheart till dawn.

Detail of an 8-metre painting for UNITAS hospital, Pretoria. The 4 panels each represented a letter in the word LIVE. There was an infantile outcry about some bathing nudes and it was removed & sold to 2 separate collectors. KB disowned it.

Jellyroll Sam Mbabala, assistant chef & handyman at restaurant & HQ, caught in his favourite spot, KB's

MEALIEPAP

DECADENT PAP

Pap & caviar have always been representative of the ups & downs of the artist's life of your token peasant Kitchenboy. It doesn't matter how much you have on your table, but the way you see & eat it adds quality to your life or subtracts from it. To our discredit our country and continent have never accorded pap the reverence an Oriental has for a simple bowl of rice. Neither have we managed to elevate it above the mundane, as the Italians did with polenta.

Armed with the previous pap recipes, try the following variations or go crazy with your own well-aimed combinations:

SOFT PORRIDGE

(aka slappap). Stir in some dried fruit & nuts, or savoury bits of cooked or cured meat, egg, vegetables & herbs. Flavour further with a little sesame oil. Incidentally, biltong tastes horrible thus.

WET PORRIDGE OR POLENTA

Serve it wet with a pasta sauce or just a topping of Parmesan or gorgonzola cheese (heated with mascarpone or cream). Especially good with game. Or float as an island for grilled meats with a flavoursome broth surrounding it. Before casting it in a flat container to set and cut in slices to fry, grill or braai, mix in some pretty bits like diced red pepper or other vegetables, peanuts & such, fermented black beans, mushrooms, chorizo, bacon or ham, and chopped herbs like parsley, basil or origanum. Serve under a salad or as a platform for grilled meats with interesting vegetables, leaves and a simple dressing or sauce.

PUTU

(aka stywepap). Formed into balls and incorporating or coating it with pretty ingredients as above, it can be wrapped like big sweets into figs or walnuts, or as couscous (*cuzcuz* is thus enjoyed in Brazil with prawns).

More as a challenge to you than an astounding new dish, I would like to provoke you into changing your attitude about the blandness of pap with this humble thingie Junglegirl & I created as a starter prepared like their *gongee*, a soupy rice dish into which morsels of meat, fish, seafood and/or vegetables are added. Enjoyed as breakfast sustenance by the majority of Chinese, particularly the poor, it is found here only on the complicated menus of *Yam Cha* (Chinese brunch).

MEALIEPAP

MEALIE MEAL CONGEE

6 cups water
1 tsp salt
¼ cup mealie meal
1 Chinese black mushroom, soaked & sliced
1 egg, lightly whisked
1 tbsp dried shrimp, pre-soaked in boiling
water for 30 minutes
3 small baby spinaches, with stems, shredded
1 tbsp dried roasted garlic flakes

- Boil the water and salt and stir in the mealie meal
in a thin rain & bring back to the boil.
- Add the mushroom and, stirring in one direction, dribble
the egg into the edge, which will cook in shreds.
- Add the shrimp, spinach & garlic flakes, and
serve forthwith.

Bedtime. KB's view up the staircase clad in taxi dashboard fur, and Junglegirl's view down.

MUSHROOMS

CHINESE BLACK MUSHROOMS

If your head is as perpetually on a gourmet cloud like your contemplating Kitchenboy, a single ingredient, like the ancient dried Chinese mushroom, can sky-rocket you off to another space, another time, aye, another planet.

Quite apart from preserving the highly perishable Chinese black mushrooms (*Lentinus edodus*), drying also magically intensifies their flavour, wisely making them virtually exclusively available in this form.

Not black at all, the best quality mushrooms are a light grey-brown buff on the cap, with a fat rim, golden gills and a small stem. The Japanese variety, *shiitake*, (aka winter mushroom in northern China) has a browner cap and thinner rim, but they can be used interchangeably. Indeed, few food writers seem to know the difference. Naturally, they have to be rehydrated before use. Pour boiling water over them and soak for 30 minutes,

keeping them submerged with a saucer or whatnot. Squeeze them dry and cut off and discard the tough stem. Chop, sliver or leave whole and beautify (traditionally) with a star on the cap. Enormously versatile, they can be used in all your soups, stews, steamed dishes, stir-fries, risottos, scrambled eggs, etc.

Your passionate **Kitchenboy**, however, loves these Chinese black mushrooms best in delicate Oriental soups or one-pot dishes. Thus they possess a plump slow-motion chewiness, which fills your mouth and mind with a skelm delight, of the sort which might cease abruptly if you are disturbed in the act.

Don't skrik yourself wet because of the exotic ingredients in my recipe. You are going to design your very own noodle pot, according to your own larder and preferences. A really tasty stock is essential, and though I use sublime Japanese *dashi* here, I often favour a mild chicken stock. But then you're on you're own, China. Any mushrooms, any seafood, any meat, any noodles and any greens (or reds for that matter). Don't hesitate to mix, say, clams & chicken or pork & fish. It's all about a composition of textures. The final trick is, as with horseriding (and other such rakish pastimes), to show noble restraint. Keep it light and don't overcrowd it with half a chicken and twenty mushrooms. Look what happened to dear old potjiekos.

A niche in the library. KB has an irreverent habit of cluttering unrelated objects together.

MUSHROOMS

UDON POT
(Udon Suki)

THE BROTH
1,5 litres water
3 tsp instant *dashi* (Japanese stock)
½ cup quality light soy sauce (i.e. Kikkoman)
½ cup *sake* (Japanese rice wine)
1 tbsp sugar
1 or 2 chillies

THE SOLIDS
dried Chinese black mushrooms, rehydrated
1 block tofu (bean curd), cubed
1 pkt fresh udon noodles, blanched
6 tiger prawns, whole & deveined
few leaves Chinese greens (*bok choy* or water spinach)
few slices Japanese fish cake (*kamabuko*) (a tasteless optional)

• First make the broth, and keep tasting as you go along. This is going to be your supreme understatement. Aim for a benign sweet-saltiness with mysterious undertones. Above all, don't darken it with too much soy sauce, just an elegant hue. Keep in mind the stock will be pregnant with all the soluble flavours of the added solids. • You may assemble the dish in the kitchen, adding the solids as listed above, according to the time they take to cook, and portion it into six deep bowls (broth to solids).
• Alternatively, if you have heat at the dining table, arrange the prepped ingredients exquisitely on a serving plate (noodles underneath, to be reheated and slurped last with the broth). Then let the diners cook-and-eat fondue style, togethel. Sorry, togethler. Togele …th …oh never mind. Just keep sipping the *sake*. Try it with ice for a change, or a flavouring of dry vermouth for a vodkatini, currently the rave dop at Kitchenboy HQ.

Natasha & Yellow Monster. Indirectly, she caused KB's swing from artist to restaurateur, when he impulsively declared himself a bachelor & moved into The Chapel, a wondrous abode in Troyeville, where he eventually opened his infamous eatery.

Ex-wife Wimpie & KB, some years later in the restaurant. She was dazzling, an ardent philosopher and a wonderful partner for 13 years. Then came the time for another life.

MUSHROOMS

ALTERNATIVE FUNGI

Only recently, in the late 60's, did your paranoid Kitchenboy's tribe overcome their deeply imprinted fear & distrust of paddastoele (toadstools), and started devouring them with unprecedented enthusiasm. How sad that so few venture beyond the flavourless little button mushrooms in meaningless steak & hamburger sauces, or limp brown vegetarian caps devastated with butter & garlic. The following ones are available commercially, and well worth the trouble of hunting further than your common supermarket shelves.

BUTTON MUSHROOMS

(aka *champignons*). Stab me in the heart please, before you give me one of those miserable sauces or soups made from these blah play-veggies grown in horse manure. Like so many mushrooms, composed mostly of water, they are much more concentrated in flavour when dried, the only way I eat them these days. Crumble finely and press a seasoned steak, chop, chicken or fish fillet into it till well coated, then fry in foaming butter till crisp & golden.

BROWN MUSHROOMS

A single note higher in flavour than the former, their mushy texture is more suitable to be added to soups & stews at the last minute than frying or grilling. Or heat through, under cover in a microwave with a squirt of soy sauce, garlic & chilli.

CEPS

(aka *porcini – Boletus edulis*). My all-round favourite mushroom for bold, meaty flavour, firm texture and keen reaction to heat. My most memorable gastronomic experience was accidentally walking into an aroma-blasted *porcini*-drying plant in Amsterdam, while fishing in the lake district around Chrissiesmeer. Back in camp, we cooked them simply and brilliantly thus: Melt a knob of butter & season with coarse black pepper, salt & finely chopped parsley. Wipe any sand & dirt off ceps (do not wash), and cut in fat slices. Fry till golden but not soft. You may add a splash of lemon, sherry, *sake* or port, but try it plain first. Fab in soups (also from dry) and casseroles, scrambled eggs & omelettes, sauces for meat, fish, rice or pasta or, stupendously, in *Risotto ai Fungi*. Reaches high-class greengrocers in the rainy season, going into a new moon, though imports also appear sporadically. Select large unbruised & unbroken ones, and check that the greenish gills (tiny tubes rather) are not soft or slimy.

OYSTER MUSHROOMS

Best of our commercially cultivated mushrooms, and quite robust despite their frail beauty. Cook like ceps or stir-fry – frying brings out the best in them. Or brush with butter or oil and cook briefly on a griddle plate or braai. Often used in soups for their beauty.

MORELS

Only seen them dried. These honeycombed cones, a favourite of European chefs, have to be thoroughly rid of sand & stones after soaking. Use in sauces for pasta or accompaniment with poultry & game or for stuffing.

CHANTERELLES

Found these delicate little yellowish umbrellas fresh for the first time on our markets last season, exorbitantly priced and riddled with sand. Rinse thoroughly in cold water and drain on a towel. Prepare simply, like ceps.

CHINESE BLACK MUSHROOMS

Never sold fresh, always dried to concentrate their subtle flavour and not black at all, but brown to pale buff. The largest, lightest ones with a highly crackled surface are the most highly prized & priced. They are sometimes elaborately packaged. But smaller, less expensive ones are as good, and they go a very long way. Soak in boiling water for 20-30 minutes, under weight to keep them submerged. Rinse to rid them of sand and strain soaking water as stock. Remove hard stem & discard, then use whole or sliced in soups, stews, steamboats or stir-fries. Delicious cooked in equal parts of soy sauce, sugar & *sake* till syrupy.

SHIITAKE

Closely related to the Chinese black mushroom, which can be

MUSHROOMS

used in its stead, the Japanese *shiitaki* is grown on the bark of shiia oaks, and is sometimes available fresh, although these have never really done much for me. Use them in soups & udon & other one-pot dishes, deep-fry for *tempura* or cook as other fresh mushrooms. Dried ones are soaked like the Chinese variety. Traditionally cross-cut on the cap for dekorasie and to allow thick part to cook through.

ENOKI MUSHROOMS
(aka Enokitake). Clumps of slender stems with tiny caps and available only canned or bottled. Queerly textured with exquisite flavour. Use it in soups & one-pots or mildly flavoured Chinese stir-fries.

CLOUD EARS
(aka wood ears, because they are grown on trees). Crumpled papery dried fungus from China & Japan. Brown or black, the best are fawn-coloured outside & black inside. They need to be soaked for 20 minutes in hot water, when they swell prodigiously – some 10 times their size – and look like seaweed. Rinse well to remove sand, cut away hard navel and slice or tear into clear soups, stews, stir-fries & egg or tofu dishes, more to add black colour & crunchy texture than their nowhere flavour. Inexpensive.

SILVER EARS
A frilly white dried fungus from China with almost no flavour and gelatinous texture. Soak in hot water for an hour, remove stalk-navel and use in sweet dishes like compotes with syrup – & to my mirth & pleasure – typically with mixed canned fruit. Inexpensive.

STRAW MUSHROOMS
Grown on paddy straw in the Orient, these quail egg-sized, brown & conical mushrooms are never dried but readily canned. Interesting musty flavour and good in soups & stews.

TRUFFLES
This is almost an embarrassing admission but truth is, all along, Kitchenboy was utterly under-whelmed by the taste of truffles. Pound for pound, he would rather be kissed by a pretty plaasmeisie, than encourage pretentious food snobbery.

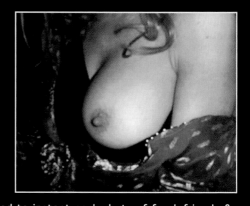

The magic of digital still cameras is not limited to instant pack shots of food, friends & parties in the life of a hedonist. KB duly built up an admirable collection of consenting boob-snatches & flashes. Recognize any? Quite a toy in the bedroom too, actually.

ASIAN NOODLES

Jaaa, ja, your backyard philosopher, Kitchenboy, will teach you to make pasta, yet. But first you get noodles, glorious Oriental noodles. Their culinary ingenuity, diversity and brilliance far outshines anything slipping around a plate in Italy, which is a poor imitation indeed.

It is easier to identify our bewildering alternatives by sight and feel, than learning to read the Chinese or Thai on the exquisitely wrapped cellophane packets lining the shelves of Asian supermarkets. Endearing as it may be, following the rare English instructions can be equally exasperating. Typically, it would go like this: 'Pour the boiled noodle suddenly subjected to the cold water.' Or, on the same packet: 'Fresh and healthy owing to the H.T. treatment and mechanical stove.'

Increasing export to the West and its import regulations, however, requires at least a listing of ingredients, which is what you'll search for. Dried, fresh, cooked, frozen or any combination of these, no matter whether thick, thin or in sheets, you first have to establish what they are composed of before you can plunge into their astounding wonderland of flavours, historical dishes and infinite creative possibilities.

WHEAT NOODLES (plain white flour-water noodles).

FRESH OR FROZEN (aka *hokkien* or Shanghai noodles). Off-white and usually quite plump, found in plastic bags in the supermarket refrigerator. Use as a side-dish with condiments, in soups, casseroles, one-pot dishes or stir-fries. The most underrated, and for me, the greatest of all noodles, Deliriously nutty when toasted (after boiling) in a little oil (don't stir for a minute or two, then flip over), before you tumble a wok-full of undercooked anything over it.

DRIED (aka *mien, mie, ramen*). Off-white bundles of round or flat ribbons or wavy instant noodles (yes those cheapskate packs, just gooi weg the trashy sachets). Use as for fresh. Most need minimal boiling.

WONTON WRAPPERS (fresh or frozen). Neat little paper parcels, big, small, round or square. Usually egg-bound, though most keep under damp cloth.

SWUNG NOODLES. For your academic enlightenment only. No offence, but nobody can emulate those acrobatic Chinese restaurant chefs, pulling lumps of fresh dough, multiplying and thinning the strands as they swing along.

SILVER PIN NOODLES (aka silver needles). Can only be hand-rolled at home from a special wheat flour, which turns transparent when cooked. It is the same dough used in that jewel of all *dim-sum*, the prawn *haw-gaw* (aka *har gau*).

often in tight but brittle one-portion bundles, and for some mysterious reason utterly and deliciously alien in taste to spaghetti. Best are the handmade bundles which look as if glued together, the fatter the better, usually loose in boxes or in unmarked packs. Patiently disentangle with a chopstick as they soften in boiling water. Err on the undercooked side. Quite robust and chewy in soups, one-pots, stir-fries & toasted. Great all-rounder and larder standby. Also in shrimp and other flavours, about which I have my reservations.

ASIAN NOODLES

E-FU NOODLES (aka golden Chinese egg noodles) cooked and deep-fried in loose pads. Need only be soaked in hot water for a minute or two to soften and float the oil out. Use in soups or braised dishes, or cold with shredded meat and spicy sauce.

COOKING NOODLES

A hangover from my restaurant days, I still like pre-cooking and cooling most noodles, specially when throwing a dinner party, having them at the ready at the last minute to serve cold and include in salads, soups, hotpots, braised dishes, stir-fries, toast-fries and deep-fries. Thus they also reheat perfectly in a minute or two under cling wrap or in a plastic bag in a microwave. Happy like that in your fridge too, for 2 or 3 days. Or freeze, from whence it's straight to the microwave again.

With rice, you get rid of the surface flour-to-become-glue by rinsing it before you cook it. With noodles you rinse the glue off afterwards, and that's why you boil it in a moerse lot of water, say five times more than you need to cover.

I never use salt. Get the water to a rolling boil, plunge the fresh, frozen or dried noodles into it and stay there, because the loose flour will definitely cause it to boil over like milk. Now don't go and burn yourself by yanking the pot off the heat. Simply blow gently on it to let the air bubbles escape. The Japanese have a rather twee remedy – they add a cup of cold water when it comes to the boil. Repeat 3 to 4 times till done.

Using a single chopstick, twirl them around patiently (untangling patiently if they are frozen or dried nests). Fish one out every minute to check for doneness (still firm but not raw in the core, and don't you dare say *al dente*). Few will take longer than 5 minutes.

Stop the cooking immediately, and wash off the glue by rinsing and draining them thoroughly in a large sieve or colander under cold running water. Toss them in a few spoons of vegetable oil to keep them slithering and to facilitate stir-frying. Since noodles symbolise longevity, never bite off a noodle to bring about your early demise, but slurp away to a long and happy life.

Kemper 99·11·15

To Junglegirl, as with everything I think & do. Love, B.

Self-portrait in Blue. Sketching in blue ink isn't just a fad. On a long fishing outing in Dullstroom, KB ran out of black, and found an old, half-evaporated bottle of Stephen's blue school ink in a shop he frequented as a boy with his oupa, who farmed nearby, on Tonteldoos.

Kitchenboy
Year of the Dragon

2000 is another favourite subject, along with monsters and other beasts.

RICE NOODLES

FRESH RICE NOODLES. Very soft & semi-translucent white in refrigerator. Made by steaming sheets of rice flour paste, to be cut by you into broad noodles. Incredibly fragile, even when steamed with prawns & things for *dim-sum*. One I never managed to crack, even the eating thereof, and thank God quite rare.

RICE VERMICELLI (aka rice stick). Brittle, wiry big wads like transparent grey to white steel wool. Much loved in Thailand and Indonesia. Astonishing metamorphosis whichever way you choose to cook it. When soaked in boiling water for 3 to 4 minutes it collapses into gelatinous, slippery transparent strands. Drain and cool to use in Thai salads with herbs, prawns & pork or whatever with an oil-free dressing, or add to soups or even stir-fries. Expands to 5 times its volume in an instant when hazardously crisply deep-fried. Test the oil with a strand, have wire scoop ready to hurriedly submerge uncovered bits (which will be inedible), stand back and whisk it out onto a paper napkin immediately (it burns in seconds). To be used as a bed for absolutely anything juicy & delicious like a South-East Asian curry or stir-fry, as in my all-time favourite Vietnamese *Pho Xai*, where the soggy parts melt away while the rest crackles undertooth, like Martian styrofoam. Goes funny when made longer than an hour ahead of serving. Typically used thus by Western chefs as a garnish, shame, to parade their food as fashionably South East Asian.

RICE STICK (aka *Banh Pho, Sha Ho Fun*). Large bundles of flat semi-transparent noodles of varying widths. Barely cook or soak in boiling water or soup for soup-noodle dishes like those from Hanoi, called *Pho*. This is also the one in the famous Thai street food *Pad Thai*. I like flash-frying a whole wad of it like the vermicelli above (flip over quickly for other side) as a bed for anything from a whole fish to various wicked stir-fries.

RICE PAPER (aka *Bahn Trang*). Not to be confused with soluble Western rice paper of nougat fame. Round or square almost transparent sheets bearing the pattern of the mats they are dried on. Incredibly fragile and brittle – look for unbroken ones and handle gently. Dip in slightly cooled boiling water till pliant and transparent. Wrap around herbs, salads and shredded meats as Vietnamese Crystal Spring Rolls with a sweet-sharp dipping sauce. Make spring rolls with rice vermicelli & vegetables or wrap around large peeled prawns and deep-fry, to dunk in a sweet chilli dip. Gorgeous things.

MUNG BEAN NOODLES

BEAN THREADS (aka cellophane noodles, glass or transparent vermicelli and jelly noodles). Bundles of vermicelli-like strands made by extruding mung bean starch. Easily confused with rice stick, which it resembles, but startlingly tough, even difficult to cut with scissors, which is why it is often packaged in one-person portions. Don't boil, simply soak in hot water for 10-15 minutes. Use in soups, stir-fries, braised dishes and hotpots. Also used in *Laksa*, that coconut milk curry soup of Indonesia.

BEAN NOODLES. Flat ribbons in bundles, treated and used as bean threads.

BEAN SHEETS (aka green bean starch sheet). Looks like large rice paper, which it is not. Soak for 30 minutes in boiling water and cut to size for wrappers.

BEAN CURD NOODLES.

BEAN CURD NOODLES, fresh (aka soy noodles and soy vermicelli). Not at all related to bean threads. Soft, brownish thick strips. Gently boil and serve soft with shredded vegetables or vegetarian hotpots, soups or cold as an appetiser.

BEAN CURD SHEETS, fresh. Large folded sheets. As above to use as wrappers or to cut as noodles. I have seen, but never used them.

BEAN CURD SKINS. Entirely different from the previous two, being the dried skin that forms on top while making tofu. Large light brown sheets, extremely brittle. Soak in cold water till pliable, then cut with scissors & use as noodles or wrappers in casseroles. Can be crisply deep-fried too.

BEAN CURD STICKS. Made as the skins, but pleated before drying. Soften by soaking, cut in pieces and use as meat substitute in vegetarian dishes. Often deep-fried.

JAPANESE NOODLES

The Japanese almost always eat

ASIAN NOODLES

their noodles with a broth or dipping sauce made of stock (*dashi*), soy sauce and *mirin*.

UDON PRE-COOKED. Very white from the special wheat starch they contain, sealed in (wormy) little packets in refrigerators, often with Japanese calligraphy. They are extensively used in Japan. They really just need to be heated through in boiling water. These noodles have a queer evasive dumpling flavour. They are perfect in a clear broth like the *dashi* of the famous udon pot and unexpectedly full of flavour when stir-fried (go on, let them stick a little).

UDON DRIED. Straight bundles of white flattish wheat-flour noodles. Cooked till just tender for Japanese soups, broths or one-pots. Chuck them in last because discolouring them is most unkind. Not as good as pre-cooked.

SOMEN. Fine white 'summer' noodles in prettily tied little bundles. They cook quite quickly – about 5 minutes. Drain, rinse and cool. Toss with raw or blanched vegetables with dressing or use as *soba*.

SOBA (aka buckwheat noodles). Buff-coloured sticks in pretty bundles, made of buckwheat & wheat flour. Simmer, don't boil, or add a cup of cold water when it does, till cooked. Rinse, cool and serve elegantly cold on ice or in a basket, topped with *tempura*, with a chilled light dipping sauce & condiments as for *sashimi*. Or serve in broth like udon pot or in the famed *sukiyaki*.

SHIRATAKI (literally 'white waterfall'). Plastic-like, pliant sticks made from an extrusion of the root of *konnyaku* or 'devil's tongue'. Soak in warm water for 5 minutes before using in *sukiyaki*. Sometimes packed in water (then rinse). Crunchy texture. Expensive.

ECCENTRIC NOODLES

PRAWN CRACKERS. Chinese transparent wafers. Deep-fry instantly to familiar wobbles of crisp puffs at tatty dip parties. Quick and oil-free on the microwave turntable.

KRUPUK. Larger and infinitely tastier from real prawn meat, if you can get them. Deep-fry and serve with peanut sauce or as garnish.

AGAR-AGAR. Look like but are not noodles at all, but seaweed jelly which should be softened before boiling. Used in jellied sweets.

Crowned by that Gordon's Vodka logo which KB regularly copied as an art student, and an early symbol of his love for rude dop & getting drunk.

PASTA

HANDMADE PASTA

As a kaalvoet outjie, your once innocent Kitchenboy and his hare-hunting mongrel whippet would burst into a carefree trot through the veld to the nearby Blesbokspruit, sporting a fishing rod in one hand and in the other, nimbly kneading an egg-flour paste for bait. He has been making pasta like that ever since.

FLOP-FREE HANDMADE PASTA

Refer to step-by-step kiekie-comic
For every guest: 1 extra-large free-range egg. I cup cake flour (I prefer bread flour or even semolina for a tougher, chewier pasta).

BY FOOD PROCESSOR

Though not necessary, a food processor is a lightning-fast & clean shortcut. (A) Just dump the flour, then the egg in the bowl. Switch on fast for one minute.There is a trick to it though, Under no circumstances may it form a solid ball swivelling berserkly around the blade shaft. (B) Aim at a moist but loose texture like couscous or krummelpap. Squeezing it all together, though, it should form a dense mass. Continue from step 3

BY HAND

(1) Plop the flour in a peaked heap onto a large work surface or bowl. Dent a hollow at the top, volcano-style. Break the eggs into this well.
(2) With your two naughty fingers and a loose wrist, twiddle the goo around in a circular motion, allowing the flour to gather naturally to the muck on your fingers. Carry on till you have a messy but firm ball of dough – the firmer, the better the pasta. (3) Chuck it into a plastic bag or cling wrap. Knead the dough ball inside the plastic till more or less amalgamated. (4) Let it rest thus for at least an hour. I secretly believe it allows the grains to absorb the moisture and so ease the kneading

PASTA

KNEADING BY HAND

Keep at it till you have shiny, uniform dough. If too dry, moisten a little, and if too sticky, flour up your hands. It should take about 10 minutes of Zen therapy. On a floured board, roll out into thin sheets. Dust the surface with flour again.

KNEADING BY PASTA MACHINE

Not essential, but probably the best reason for buying one. (5) Just flatten a tennisball-sized bit of dough and wind it through the widest setting of the flat rollers. Fold it double, dust with flour if it gets sticky, and crank trough again. Repeat twice or so until the floury streaks disappear. Narrowing the roller setting each time, feed the sheet through repeatedly till the desired thickness is achieved (I prefer the second-last setting).

Cutting the sheets: cut into squares or rectangles for wonton wrappers, ravioli, lasagne or whatnot. Or roll up and cut into thin or wide noodles with a sharp knife and unravel the strands. (6) Or feed through the cutting rollers of a pasta machine. (7 + 8) Handling the strands carefully, separate them and hang them over a broomstick, dowel or wooden coat hanger to dry for an hour. Check that the strands do not overlap or they will stick together while cooking.

COOKING PASTA

Remember how we made glue for our kites or *papier-mâché* with flour & water? You don't want glue in this instance, so get a really big pot of water to a rolling boil. Oh, and don't add oil, it's pure myth that it will separate the pasta -- it floats on top anyway. But add plenty of salt. Not only will it season the pasta but it will raise the boiling temperature considerably. Let the pasta slide from the stick into the water and let it return to the boil. All that flour (read 'glue') is going to trap the air/steam bubbles wanting to escape and cause it to boil over. For God's sake don't jerk the pot off the heat and risk burning yourself, and don't turn down the heat – just blow on it gently and the bubbles will escape. Twirl the strands around with long chopsticks or a roasting fork to keep them separate and cook till barely done but not raw inside. *Al dente* se gat. Immediately drain into a colander and serve with your favourite topping.

PASTA

KITCHENBOY'S NEW WAVE PASTA

Kitchenboy is seriously gatvol of those generic Italianate sauces traditionally paired with pasta and prefers a more creative, contemporary approach, even at the risk of being simply trendy.
Toasting gives a marvellous new dimension to pasta.
Just toss in butter and grill, pan-fry or wok-fry it till it acquires some blotchy colour on the outside.
Assemble some fresh vegetables & grill or stir-fry very briefly onto a nest of toasted noodles, with or without some sliced grilled meat of your choice, and generously rain torn herbs and black pepper over it.

Wet with this simple but stunning dressing:
½ cup extra-virgin olive oil
2 tbsp balsamic vinegar
1 tbsp honey

St Lucia, where an unimpressed Junglegirl met a pissed & obnoxious KB,
through her boyfriend.

Kitchenboy

POTATOES

BOILING

No food on or under the earth offends your pretentious Kitchenboy as much as the hideous potato – even its vulgar name has the poet in him dying. But he is also the first to snatch a roast potato from the oven, dig into a velvety mash or bite through a golden croquette, for few foods alter personality as willingly as this Cinderella of the vegetable world.

The tubers of this relative of tobacco, tomato & deadly nightshade can be poisonous. When exposed to sunlight, they not only produce green chlorophyll & start growing, they also develop toxic levels of alkaloids, which aren't destroyed by heat and are concentrated around the sprouting eyes. That's why they should be stored in the dark and if starting to turn green, should be deeply peeled and the eyes gouged out. Perhaps this too is why I so despise potatoes in their skins.

Unsightly browning on peeled potatoes (or apples, bananas, etc) is caused by an oxidising enzyme which is inhibited by acids such as ascorbic acid (vitamin C) found in lemons; in fact, investigating this phenomenon was how vitamin C was discovered. But simply covering them with water will rob them of oxygen & retard discolouring.

The myriad varieties now available can be distinguished by their floury or waxy texture. Floury ones are best for stewing, mashing, baking, roasting & deep-frying. Waxy ones, such as new potatoes, keep their shape better, but with my luck every other one turns out to be glassy. Dropping them into a brine of salt & water (1:11) is the only foolproof way to tell (floury potatoes will float), but clearly this procedure is a bit awkward in a supermarket aisle.

Few nations understand boiling floury potatoes as well as the Portuguese, who use them to thicken their national kale soup, *caldo verde,* or boil them to a point just before implosion & serve them with *bacalhau* or their rustic stews. Touching the large pale spheres with a fork is often enough to collapse them into the sauce. Even cold, these are gorgeous in *vichyssoise,* the leek & potato soup invented by a French-American chef. We Boertjies call floury potatoes *blusaartappels* (as in 'crumble' or 'disintegrate') and they are obligatory in that Free State classic, *skaapkop & pootjies* (sheep's head & trotters), thus thickening the rich & unctuous stew. Afrikaans poet C. Louis Leipoldt curiously suggested lopping off two ends of a potato and boiling it in seawater, which I found far too salty, but interesting nonetheless.

Apart from sneaking a potato from a cold leftover stew, my most passionate, consoling boiled potato is invariably of the mashed variety, perhaps because I find it so damn hard to make it flawlessly. And very chic it has become too, as an island for designer toppings, with variations like pesto or other herb pastes, spices like saffron or ground pepper, extra-virgin olive oil, roasted garlic or Parmesan & other decent cheeses.

Robert Brozin, CEO of Nando's, with Mimi Jardim, the great authority on Portuguese cooking in SA, who directly inflamed KB with knowledge & a passion for Portuguese food. Both have had intimate ties with Nando's for many years.

POTATOES

SAFFRON MASHED POTATO

1 kg floury potatoes, peeled & washed
a generous pinch saffron
½ cup milk
½ cup butter
freshly grated nutmeg
fine white pepper

• Cut potatoes in thick, even slices and boil in salted water till very, very tender, even falling apart. • Drain off water & return to heat to drive off excess water & to remain warm while mashing. • Infuse saffron in hot milk. • Mash potatoes with fork, masher, food mill or potato ricer, but never in a food processor, which will convert them to useless goo. • Slowly add milk, then butter & seasoning while beating steadily.

Dining in the extensive KB cookbook library on a daring Junglegirl's Steak Tartare. She is his 1st partner not in the least intimidated by his kitchen antics.

An etching from the *Laatnagvrese* suite of 35, with digital hamburger & slap chips, o
course. KB's brother Cois once visited him to proudly show a conservative antie from
Potchefstroom around the studio. Too close to back off when he noticed the breasts &
fanny on the horse, he swung around and asked: "So how do you like her headlights?"

POTATOES

DEEP-FRYING

Slap chips are haughtily dismissed as junk fodder of the gastronomically feeble, but your token peasant Kitchenboy holds it in the same esteem as other great culinary inventions. The art of frying potatoes requires knowledge, understanding and a perfect sense of timing.

French fries (aka *pommes frites*, potato chips or, most romantically, slap chips) are credited to the French, but the term was first used by a Yank in 1894, claiming the US gave it to the French. However, having once lived on the breadline as an artist in the streets of Antwerp, I can duly testify to the infinite superiority of the Flemish *fritte*. To the uninitiated, I will concede, their addicting partiality to serving it in a paper cone topped with a blob of home-made mayonnaise (really just emulsified oil), exactly defeats the purpose of keeping oil out of the potato. Frying in flavourless vegetable oils can't compare with French pan-frying of potato rounds in goose or duck fat or English quartered potatoes basted with fat from the Sunday roast and the ultimate chip of Belgium, deep-fried in suet (beef kidney fat), which has a higher smoking point than other fats. But the real secret of perfect chips lies in frying them twice.

The whole point of cooking potatoes is to let the starch molecules gelatinise (@ 163 °C – 188 °C), at which point the granules lose their tightly packed structure and become fragile as they absorb water, but oppas, also oil. The frantic foaming & sputtering of chips in hot oil is caused by escaping moisture (steam), and treacherous as this may be, it is also a very desirable sign. Water & oil don't mix, and

POTATOES

if they stop emitting bubbles, it means they are absorbing oil.

SLAP CHIPS

(aka as British chips & Belgian *fritte*). Hand-cut thick sticks, rinse in water to remove surface starch and dry thoroughly on a dishcloth to prevent spattering. Deep-fry twice, a handful at a time as described above. Sprinkle with sea salt. For *fritte* serve with home-made mayonnaise.

VARIATIONS:

FRENCH FRIES (aka *pommes frites*). Cut thin sticks, rinse, dry & fry as above.
MATCHSTICKS. Even thinner than the former. Rinse, dry & fry once till crisp.
STRAW POTATOES (aka shoestring potatoes). Finely grate on rotary grater, rinse, dry & fry once till crisp.
POTATO BASKETS. Grate like shoestrings, clamp unwashed layer between two metal sieves and fry till crisp & golden.
POMMES SOUFFLÉS. Dust thin slices with flour & deep-fry till they puff up.
POTATO CRISPS (aka game chips). Slide potatoes on a mandolin into plain slivers or on the fluted blade for crinkle-cut discs, dry and fry till golden.
WAFFLE POTATOES (aka *gaufrettes*). Turn potato 90° with every cut on the fluted blade of a mandolin. Fry like crisps.

I am still in mourning after the demise of crisply crumbed croquettes served with feathered game and yes, those kitschy piped borders on the silver platters of bygone smart restaurants. And the trashy side of me (blush) still pines for an abomination made by my childhood café, a fat croquette hiding a red Vienna sausage in the core, called a sputnik.

POTATOES

POTATO CROQUETTES

1 kg potatoes, cooked & mashed (see page 197)
2 egg yolks
flour for dusting
1 whole egg, beaten
breadcrumbs

- While still warm, whisk in the egg yolks.
  Spread out on a plate to cool completely.
- Form fingers, balls or patties, dust with flour,
  dip in egg & roll in crumbs.
- Deep-fry gently till golden. Drain on paper towel.
- Serve with feathered game or venison, particularly
  with sweet fruit sauces.

Elegant & sparkling actress Tina Illman, whose intelligence & genuine talent will certainly bring the accomplishments she is seeking abroad. KB at her birthday party.

Basmati   Thai fragrant   Short-grain   Arborio

W A S H   W A S H

W A S H   W A S H

Any amount   Rinse   Till clear

Measure   Boil   Lid ajar   Fluff

For years KB has been conducting a vendetta against parboiled (converted) and in particular, Tastic rice. He recently learnt it was invented many centuries ago in southern India, and is far more nutritional than plain polished rice. This is his official apology to Tastic. He even bought a packet.

Ou Bes, darling mother of KB. As a child he so despised her old-fashioned nat rys, that he started cooking it himself. That's how it all began. Naturally she was delighted when Tastic hit the shelves. Cooks perfectly every time, no shit.

RICE

PERFECT RICE EVERYTIME

Your child prodigy Kitchenboy used to throw all his cutlery out of his cot when his rice was badly cooked, and mashed it up with his sweet pampoen (not unlike *risotto*), to wolf it down and deserve his pudding. Ou Bes, exasperated mother of the monster, heaved a sigh of relief when Tastic rice cornered the SA rice market. Fantastic Tastic, cooks perfectly every time. But once he grew into a pretentious restaurant reviewer, he would inflate like an overfed frog, in horror, when served those tasteless plastic pebbles of parboiled rice to accompany his otherwise eminently edible food.

So many delicious old types of rice are being reintroduced to the market, and it is a real pity that its wonders are explored by so few of my acquaintances and even fewer restaurants. We got the word 'rice' courtesy of Afghan *vrize*, via Iran to Greek *ruza*, to Latin *oryza* and so on and so forth into Europe. There are two main species of rice, the African *Oryza glaberrima* and the Asiatic *Oryza sativa*. We use only *Oryza sativa*, which can be grouped into three major strains: long-grain, short-grain and glutinous types.

LONG-GRAIN RICE
(aka *Indica*, a sub-species of *Oryza sativa*).

BASMATI RICE (Hindi for fragrant). Very narrow grain grown in the foothills of the Himalayas. Arguably the most enchanting rice in the world – when cooking, it perfumes your kitchen with the aroma of nuts & sandalwood. Traditionally used with curries and pilafs, but a stunning all-rounder.

THAI FRAGRANT RICE (aka jasmine rice). A gorgeous rice, my personal everyday choice. Light, fluffy and, indeed, with the faint fragrance of jasmine. Used with most South East Asian dishes. Salt is never used.

CAROLINA RICE (aka Patna rice & American white rice). Grown all over the world, this is the common rice we all know (and from which Tastic is converted). Rather bland without salt or stock, it also benefits from toasting in a little

RICE

butter or oil before boiling. Still, streets ahead of parboiled rice when cooked from scratch.

SHORT-GRAIN RICE
(aka *japonica*, another sub-species of *Oryza sativa*).

SHORT-GRAIN WHITE RICE Oval grains which are stickier than the long-grain when cooked, making it easier to eat with chopsticks. It is also used for making *congee*, a breakfast rice porridge from Southern China. Popular in Japan, this is the famous *sushi* rice. Never salted. Available from Oriental shops, often under the name of Calrose rice.

ARBORIO RICE. Named after the Italian town in the Vercelli area, where it was developed in 1946. A large fat grain with an opaque heart. It readily absorbs moisture and cooks to a soft creamy consistency, which makes it ideal for risotto. Do note that there are at least another nine Italian varieties used for risotto, all hybridised from the previous rice. Available from Italian delis.

PUDDING RICE. A ubiquitous name for a grain which goes soft & mushy when cooked into sweet rice puddings, the main use for rice in England before WWII. Also used for Flemish *rystpap*.

GLUTINOUS RICE
(Contains no gluten, by the way.)

WHITE GLUTINOUS RICE (aka sticky rice). A matt white long-grain rice, which has to be soaked for at least 3 hours, then steamed to become sweet & sticky. Used in baking, confectionery and steamed dishes.

BLACK GLUTINOUS RICE (aka black sticky rice). An unpolished rice. More burnt red than black. Used for divine desserts in Indonesia, the Philippines and Thailand, often paired with coconut milk and sugar. Soak for a minimum of 2 hours before use.

BROWN RICE (aka unpolished rice). Needs longer cooking time and more water to soften the hull. Despite anaemic health fanatics' praise, even the poorest of the poor in China won't have it on their table. Ditto KB.

WILD RICE. Spindly black seed like blackjacks. A grass and not a rice at all. Ridiculously expensive, tasteless and utterly overrated. I would be very happy to have part in its demise.

 RICE

PERFECT REAL RICE EVERY TIME

- Put any amount of long-grain or short-grain rice in a pot.
- Rinse it thoroughly under cold running water till all cloudiness disappears, which is really rice flour glue that would stick bad rice together and burn to the bottom. It may take a minute or two but this is important. I lazily leave the pot under a running tap for 5 minutes until the waters runs clear.
- Immaterial of the size of the pot or the amount of rice, cover the rice with cold water, up to the first joint of your index finger. I promise you it works.
- Bring the rice & water to a rapid boil, then turn the heat to its very lowest setting and cover it with the lid just slightly ajar, to let a little steam escape.
- If this was written in Braille, I would advise you not to look but listen when the rice at the bottom runs dry and starts to pop & crackle – a sign that all moisture has been absorbed. Take it off the heat and keep the lid on tightly till serving.

Variation: First fry the rice in a little oil or butter until it starts popping, before adding salted water or stock. This is especially good with long grains like Basmati.

Tiny painting, a take on *The Rape of Europa*, abducted on *nigiri sushi*. KB couldn't have said it better. The stubbornness of the West to learn from Asia made him take sides.

The Fairy, exquisite, scarily bright and by far KB's most cherished bouncing board on all matters food & art. He resisted all temptations of falling in love when she worked at KB, the company. But Flash, his assistant, didn't. Flash & The Fairy got married and opened their runaway success: *Superbonbon, Mighty Restaurant of Wondrousness*. He was broken-hearted over the loss of both of them.

SUSHI RICE

So much mystique & romance has been generated around the making of *sushi*, and while agreeing that it gets easier with practice, your laconic Kitchenboy really can't see what the fuss is about, or why *sushi* has to be so expensive. After all, it is just finger food or snack food, picnic food even; the Japanese equivalent of the canapé or dainty sandwich of the sixties, using rice instead of bread.

Short-grain white rice (aka Japonica) is the preferred rice of the chopstick-eating Far East, with the exception of India & Thailand, precisely because its stickiness makes it easier to pick up in little clusters. Most recipes will tell you to wash the rice till the water runs clear (which is essential to long-grain rice cooking). But when it comes to *sushi* rice, I tend to sneak a little by leaving some 'glue' in the water (read cloudiness) after 5 or so washes, to give the rice better adhesive qualities. The rice is flavoured afterwards with a rice vinegar-sugar-salt mixture, differing from other rice recipes we know in that it is introduced after cooking, and not during. That's not all. You may well make a gat of yourself if trying it the first time with an audience, but a docile assistant is highly recommended unless you have an electric fan. This makes the rice glossy.

There are no traditional formulas for the *sushi* vinegar that flavours the rice. I have never encountered two identical formulas. In fact, my *sushi* master showed me a few dozen of them, and like flavouring other food, it is pretty much a case of your own taste. So go ahead – add more sugar if you like, or less salt, but keep in mind the rice is unsalted.

Equestrian portraits are a favourite
genre. Here TV director
Pieter Cilliers
straddles the
stallion.
The
plump
hands of
KB, with
trade-mark red
Cutex, rubber-stamped at
a rave: V.I.P. & a purple kiss.

RICE

SUSHI RICE

2½ cups short-grain rice
½ cup rice vinegar (nothing else will do)
5½ tbsp sugar
1 tbsp salt

- Immaterial of the size of the pot or the amount of rice, cover the rice with cold water, up to the first joint of your index finger.
- Bring the rice & water to a rapid boil, then turn the heat to its very lowest setting and cover with the lid just slightly ajar, to let a little steam escape.
- Meanwhile, make the *sushi* vinegar by boiling the vinegar, sugar & salt, & stir till the sugar melts. Cool it rapidly in a bowl on ice.
- When the rice is fully cooked, after about 20 minutes, dump it all onto a wooden tray or tub, which helps absorb some of the moisture – what the next acrobatic activity is all about.
- DO NOT use all the *sushi* vinegar at once. While someone waves like crazy with a newspaper or hat, or an electric fan aimed directly to the tray of rice, add just enough of the liquid to moisten the rice. Using a wooden paddle (I use a square piece of plywood), rapidly cut in the liquid, trying at the same time to air the rice to let the excess moisture evaporate. Keep on going, adding a little more liquid. It will take about 10 minutes, but never allow the rice to get soggy. Cool & cover with a damp cloth till ready to use.

Although your wily **Kitchenboy** is well equipped in the art of making
sushi (recently commissioned by Penguin to write *KB on Sushi*) it is
too vast a subject for this column. He strongly recommends you learn
as he did, visiting *sushi* bars, ordering the type of *sushi* you are interested
in and watching the *sushi* master's sleight-of-hand closely.
Then fight with him about his rice.

An unusually large watercolour, *Selfportrait with Olympia* (SA National Gallery, CT). The day after KB painted it he could hardly walk from all the stretching. Then he made a pass at someone at a party & she asked what's wrong with him. "I painted a watercolour." She burst out laughing and drifted away.

Equestrian portrait of Bridget Oppenheimer, commissioned by daughter Mary Slack. KB did a companion piece of her husband Harry. But having seen too many old paintings split in two, he has a rigid fear of painting two spouses on one work.

TOFU

Of all the food known to your enlightened Kitchenboy, none achieves humbleness in the way that tofu does. And none has been more misunderstood and mangled in the Western kitchen, further spoilt by the fantastical health claims by anaemic health freaks.

Bean curd is called *tofu* in Japan & *doufu* in China, where it was invented during the Han Dynasty (206 BC to AD 220). Because of its nutritious & cheap protein, it became known as 'meat without bones'.

I have been fascinated by this curious food for many years, but despite my best shots I could never crack the art of making it at home. I used to buy mine from a tiny illegal backyard operation in Troyeville. I watched how they soaked the yellow soy beans overnight and then ground them up in a rickety contraption, before mixing with water and boiling it to a froth in a large cauldron. After cooling it a bit and straining through muslin, the resulting soy milk is curdled with gypsum (calcium sulphate, yep, also used in plaster of Paris). Nigari (magnesium chloride), a by-product of making salt from seawater, is preferred by purists and health stores, but other coagulants like Epson salts & lemon juice also work.

When the curds have settled, they are drained & left in large cloth-lined wooden trays. A plank lid helps to firm it some more, after which it is turned onto a board, cut into even blocks and stored in buckets of water as you find it in Chinese grocers.

SOFT, FRESH OR SILKEN TOFU
Made as described above, these snow-white squares with a texture of velvety blancmange have no taste or flavour at all, though I find

them slightly chalky when raw. Weird stuff indeed. But tofu readily takes on the flavour of anything it is cooked with, most famously in the pungent *Ma Po Doufu* (as immortally invented by the humble pock-marked woman for the Emperor, which is exactly what it means: the tofu of the pock-marked woman). But it is incredibly fragile and breaks up easily, which is why I like to firm it a little before using. I stand it under a board or plate at a slight angle for an hour or two.

Because soft tofu contains so much water, it is perfectly suited to suspend in soups, one-pots and stews, like the gorgeous clear & *miso* soups of Japan. Or briefly boiled to remove the raw taste, drain & serve cooled cubes with little garnishes of grated ginger and daikon radish, bonito flakes, red & white *miso*, snipped *nori*, minced spring onion, and a dipping sauce of soy sauce & lemon juice (1:1).

Slabs of tofu can be painted with *teriyaki* sauce and grilled with a sweetened *miso* paste to make ice-lolly-like *dengaku*. Roll cubes in cornflour and deep-fry to serve with grated chilli daikon and a dip of soy sauce, *mirin* and *dashi* (4:4:1)

PRESSED TOFU
Like large flat squares of white chocolate, it is fresh tofu from which the moisture has been

Kind & unselfish Selwyn Bron, of Nando's, has mothered KB about understanding the business world. He failed, but not for a lack of trying.

extensively used in soups, stews & stir-fries as in *pad thai*.

TOFU SKINS (aka *yuba*). Made from the skin that forms

grance to vegetables & braised dishes. I sometimes have a little of the red variety on its own or with rice, but beware, it is an acquired taste.

Melodrama (aka Skye Hart) dazzling and flirtatious, always stylishly dressed and an excellent chef. Helped KB set up the restaurant and often assists him with functions.

This gaping selfportrait was done as a joke. During a shoot on *KB the artist*, he was given this costume and requested to paint. He pretended to look in a mirror with the expression of a very youthful Rembrandt etching.

OLD WORLD FRUIT

DRIED FRUIT COMPOTE

When your old-hat Kitchenboy reminisces about stealing peaches in his boy-hood, he can still feel the fear in his trembling shorts, as he sat perching high in a kaalperske tree in the dead of night, frantically chucking fruit between his shirtfront and his pounding heart. His floundering virginity, too, was prema-turely lost in the dark under an old peach tree, thus making peaches pre-dictably central to his being.

The peach is indigenous to China, but the West first encountered the fruit when it had spread as far as Persia and named it accordingly: in Greek *melon persikon* and Latin *malun persicum*, as in Persian apple. From there the word sneaked into virtually every language – Italian *pesca*, French *pêsche* (from whence it was stolen by English as peach in the 14th century), Dutch *perzik* and of course, my Afrikaans perske. But call it what you may, many of the peaches I knew as a laaitie have all but disappeared from the market, edged out by the competi-tion of exotic fruits and 'improved' cultivars, pest-resistant hybrids and

farming techniques. What hap-pened, I wonder, to my smooth, maroon-skinned and lemonade-like white-fleshed kaalperske (naked peach)? When I saw my first orange-meated nectarine in New York in 1978 I was quite startled, and I still don't get excited about its acrid taste.

There was also a cream-tinted peach, a white *parvie*, as large as your fist, growing and bearing pro-lifically in our backyard, with unfor-gettably gorgeous white peach-pear meat, apparently with fine canning qualities. SA canned yellow peaches must rank among the best fruit canned anywhere, firm & tasty

OLD WORLD FRUIT

despite the rigours of those high temperatures. Cooking fruit in a syrup like that is technically a compote, like the recipe herewith, and the preferred type is the cling peach – a peach whose pulp adheres to the stone as opposed to freestone peaches, whose flesh comes away from the stone. Hans Kruger, my pa, was something of a peach expert and he was adamant that Oom Sarel is the prince of yellow peaches. He grew up in Tonteldoos (literally 'tinderbox') near Dullstroom, in the heart of geelperske country. And yes, I still giggle when I say it. Interestingly, mampoer, always made from soft fruit and not grape, like witblits, was named after Mampuru, a historical Pedi chief from the district. My oupa Abraham had extensive fruit orchards and I still clearly recall tastes of particular cultivars of peaches, pears, apples, plums & prunes, which have since vanished from my world. Oh, and there was the rambling vine of slippery

sweet marbles of flesh which popped out of the small black catawba grapes when you squeezed them into your mouth, which I have never seen for sale. Oupa would patiently sit on the stoep and peel a peach with his knipmes in one unbroken coil of skin, a feat I still emulate to this day. But his real weakness was for figs, which he zealously ripened individually under the cotton purses which once held his gunpowder-strength Horseshoe tobacco, to protect them from the finches.

But what fascinated me most on our farm with its abundance of fruit, were the racks upon racks of sliced fruit dehydrating on mesh racks in the airy, open-sided drying shed. When stewed, these would traditionally be served at breakfast or with game.

This delicious recipe was given to me by charming Beatrice Barnard, as served in the dining room of the Andries Stockenstrom Guesthouse in Graaff Reinet.

OLD WORLD FRUIT

DRIED FRUIT COMPOTE

500 g mixed dried fruit
½ bottle white muscadel
½ cup sugar
5 pods cardamom, crushed
1 quill cinnamon
3 cloves

- Mix all and soak overnight.
- Bake in an open casserole @ 200 °C(400 °F)
for 40 minutes, stirring occasionally.

On set in St Lucia: *Spotted Grunter with Prawns*, wrapped & baked in wild
banana leaves, accompanied by a pineapple-green papaya salsa.

MEMORIES

Kitchenboy

Kruger '92

Commissioned for the cover of Jeanne Goosen's novel, *Not All of Us*, KB used new girlfriend Grethe Fox as model. The movie on the screen is from their personal mythology. There was an eerie presence in those old smoke-filled flicks and particularly the look in the usherette's eyes, which still haunts him from the matinées in Nigel's Grand Theatre Bioscope.

CRÈME BRÛLÉE

In a distant existence, when your forlornly romantic Kitchenboy was just a humble painter, before this pretentious food thing took over, he associated his art works with events, experiences & people around him at that particular time. They were always far more biographically significant than the technical & philosophical twaddle the art world so shamelessly indulges in to lend weight to inferior works. And so it still is with food. Each dish is a little ear-mark in his diary.

As a gourmet peasant of the Breughel variety, my first true love was art school sweetheart, Barbara Dreyer. I still glow with memories when I cruise through Pretoria. But it was the women who shared their daily lives with me who gave me free reign in the kitchen. What I thrived on in my steady relationships, was what my laid-back lifestyle as an artist and interest in food allowed me: all the planning, buying & preparation. The role reversal thing, I guess – to welcome her home, put up her feet (I like feet), pour her a glass of wine and spoil her rotten till an exquisite dinner is served by candlelight. I like candles. All the while, glass after glass, gossiping & talking about the highs & lows of our days, our passion and our dreams. But each darling had her own eccentricities, which I had to slyly outmanoeuvre in my endeavour to please and bring quality to her life.

Wimpie Cilliers, my greatest love of all, would forever spy on the amount of oil I used, minding her nimble figure, but freshly smoked gamefish would invariably melt her at the knees. Grethe Fox, oh precious & vulnerable Grethe, had a passion for salads and inspired my commercial Girlfriend Dressings, and could be soothed with an Oriental steamed fish. Gentle princess Lynn Radford would have no pork or red meat, but would salivate over dark-fleshed wild duck, fired in clay in our kitchen hearth. And the wild, bewitching Isabella Smook, who lived on cauliflower & broccoli when I met her, took to delicately cooked seafood with abandon.

But it was to be fellow artist, The Fairy, my secret love so often featured between these lines, who became my gastronomical twin and equal on every conceivable level. The edges of innovation and outrageousness are often so fused that we forget who the originator was. To celebrate the opening of her first restaurant, even if I think she's crazy, but knowing all cooks have to do it, I asked for her most favourite recipe, in her own peculiar tongue:

'I seethe & simmer at the twisted obscene versions of great classic retro dishes that we're fobbed off with. Closest to my heart, the misunderstood Crème Brûlée. So here it is – the way God intended it.'

Bird's custard & jelly is permanently imprinted on KB. Here he bribed the hospital staff for a helping, while visiting his ailing Pa Hans. He once remarked of his first born: "One realizes you are ageing when your son is going grey and needs a wig."

MEMORY FOOD

THE FAIRY'S
CRÈME BRÛLÉE
(Burnt Cream)

4 egg yolks
2½ cups single cream
3 dessertspoons castor sugar
vanilla pod
castor sugar for topping
NOTHING ELSE

- Beat yolks into cream thoroughly, then mix in sugar.
- Add vanilla pod.
- On a double boiler, stir mixture constantly till thickness
of pouring custard, remove vanilla & pour into ramekins.
Or – the simpler route (the only deviation allowed):
Bake @ 140 °C in a large dish or individual ramekins,
placed in a bain-marie, until soft-jelly firmness
(30–40 minutes depending on container size).
- When cool, sprinkle lightly with castor sugar, place under
grill/salamander till sugar is dark brown.
- Serve chilled, not with the topping still warm.

If your topping is an ice-cap thick layer that you have to punch with
a spoon, then it is wrong, see?
Less is more & all that.

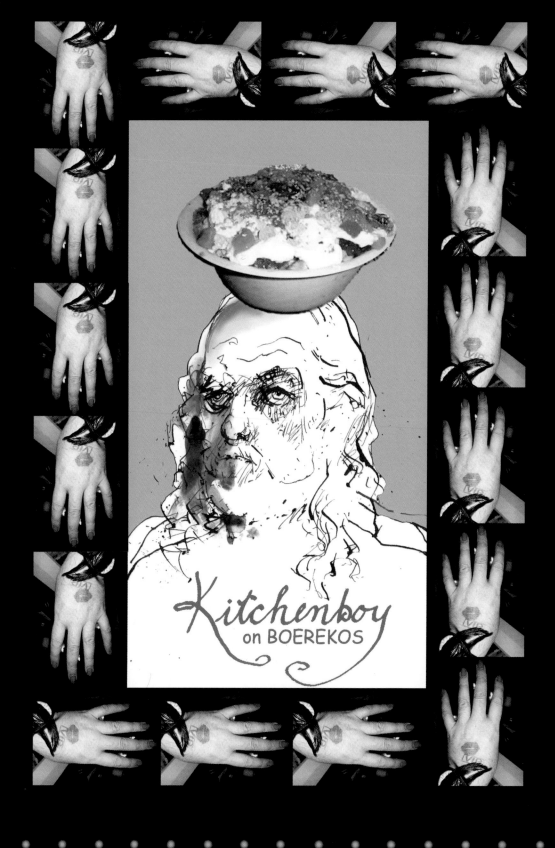

Kitchenboy
on BOEREKOS

SOUSKLUITJIES

It is with a chuckle of endearment that your opstoker Kitchenboy thinks about the Boerekos of his tribe. Most of them would hate to think that the culinary legacy of the Voortrekkers is really just a hangover from the Engelse kos they encountered on the Eastern Cape border under decades of British rule. The only cooking manuals around at the time of their exodus were English too. Goeiemôre, Mrs. Beaton.

The Boerekos encountered in upcountry Afrikaans homes is invariably of the roast or stew & 3-veg variety: heaps of overcooked meat, rice and potatoes and grey, mushy vegetables & gravy, finished off with a steamed pudding, trifle and other such skottels (dishes) which gave British cooking such a bad reputation. It thus became the dreaded mainstay of our cheap hotels, boarding houses & canteens. Right down to koek-en-tee. Why, my oupa Abraham, who hated the English from his concentration camp memories, even slurped his tea from the saucer, a habit they picked up in colonial India. My pa, Hans Kruger, died peacefully a while ago. He was an upright, honest man, a model citizen and family man with an intellect I sincerely admired. Ever since I have been searching for a food connection around which I could weave a tribute of sorts to my old man. Maybe I was just searching whence this food madness of mine came from, because from Ou Bes, my darling mom, it certainly didn't (a repeated statement she deeply resents). Haai maar wragtig Ma, Boerekos-of-de-not, you're just not the domesticated type. To my confusion I couldn't remember a single dish dear to him, so I phoned Ou Bes. She too said he hated fish, despised chicken and basically wasn't a food lover at all. After a rethink she phoned to say that she could seduce him with a simple plate of *melkkos* or *souskluitjies*, Sunday supper dishes I regularly pine for. Now Ou Bes may not have been born with a pot in her hand, except when it comes to poerring (pudding), the best cloying roly-poly, melktert, trifle, chocolate-koek, and of course her famed souskluitjies. Inevitably, it was time for Bes to

meet Junglegirl, my youthful partner, and on this occasion she duly demonstrated the art of making proper souskluitjies. All I could remember of it from my childhood was the holler from the kitchen: 'Moenie die deksel oplig nie, hulle gaan toeslaan!' (Don't remove the lid, they'll implode!) This then, is her recipe. Junglegirl tested it; KB's imploded.

Playboy S.A. was great fun while it lasted. Editor Paul Kerton & Assistant Editor Shona Bagley & Food Editor, Kitchenboy, who has lost much weight since then. He has simply learnt to eat less, because it's blerrie true: eating makes you fat.

BOEREKOS

OU BES SE SOUSKLUITJIES

1 tbsp soft butter
1 tbsp sugar
1 pinch of salt
6 heaped tbsp cake flour
1 tsp baking powder
1 egg
1 tbsp milk
3 cups water
cinnamon
sugar

• Mix the soft butter with the sugar & salt.
• Sift the flour & baking powder. • Whisk egg & milk together.
• Add egg to butter-sugar mixture, alternating with flour,
& rub to a fairly firm, loose dough. • Bring water to a boil in a heavy,
tight-lidded saucepan & remove from heat.
• Drop teaspoonfuls of the mixture into the hot water, slam the lid
on very tightly and return to the heat. For God's sake don't lift the
lid during cooking or else the dumplings will collapse into
inedible chewy glueballs (like mine). • Cook for 15 minutes, lift into a
warmed, lidded serving dish and dot each with butter.
• Sprinkle liberally with cinnamon & sugar, cover and serve hot or
cold. I remember them with much more watery syrup-cum-sauce and
thus add sugar to the remaining water to add to the dish.

The Dark Secret, oil on wood panel. One reason KB likes using androgynous models is that an artwork has a life of its own and can then go either way. Hell, he wouldn't mind if we were all hermaphrodites. Then there wouldn't be all this gender discrimination and we could have awesome sex, without fearing our other side. As a dear queen once

was the last of the legendary Suzettes.

A notorious fibber, Henri Carpentier, laid the unchallenged claim to inventing them, as a 14-year-old *commis de rang* at Monte Carlo's Café de Paris. In one of his several accounts, he was in charge of the table where the Prince of Wales (later Edward VII) was lunching with a lady, and invented a

It became the darling of the pompous eating circuit, where the *maitres d'hôtel* would push in a side table (*guèridon*) and cook a variety of meat, seafood and dessert dishes in front of the diners, flamboyantly flaming them. But none achieved the status and fame of the crêpe Suzette.

But first you need pancakes. Buy them or make them thus:

CRÊPES SUZETTE

PANCAKES

1 cup flour
pinch salt
¼ cup water
¾ cup milk
3 eggs
1 egg yolk
2 tbsp butter, melted
more butter for cooking pancakes

- Whisk or process the flour, salt, water & milk, then eggs, then butter to a smooth batter.
- Cover & rest for an hour.
- Heat the pan over a medium flame.
- Stir up the batter (and between each pancake).
- Butter the hot pan well and immediately pour in just enough batter on the side of the tilted pan, swirling it to cover the base, to make a very thin pancake. Err on the less-batter side. Holes will be camouflaged when folded. The first one will be a flop, guaranteed. That seasons the pan.
- Butter liberally again. Make the next one and loosen the edges with a spatula or knife and turn it over or toss it if you can.
- Cook the other side and slide it onto a large plate. Stack the others on top.
- Cover with cling wrap and set aside till needed.

CRÊPES SUZETTE

CRÊPES SUZETTE

(Makes 2 servings)
4 tbsp butter
6 tbsp sugar
4 cooked pancakes
zest of 1 orange
juice of 1 orange
3 tbsp Triple Sec Curaçao
double tot Cognac (Hennessy)

- Heat a large pan (preferably copper), melt the butter and sugar and let it caramelise a little, stirring continuously.
- Add the orange zest, orange juice and Curaçao.
- Lay the pancakes in the sauce, one by one, and fold each one twice with a fork, to form a triangle.
- Arrange the pancakes neatly in the pan and cook a minute or two till well soaked and heated through.
- Add the Cognac to the front of the pan, heat for a second to produce alcohol fumes, and tilt the front of the pan to set the alcohol on fire.
- FLAMBÉEEEEEEEEE!
- Serve immediately.

Kitchenboy & Junglegirl, late-night in their kitchen.

SOUFFLÉ

GRAND MARNIER SOUFFLÉ

Your loskop Kitchenboy recently reviewed French restaurant Ile de France on Radio 702, and aired this recipe for their exquisite Grand Marnier Soufflé. It caused an unheard of scramble to his helpline & the station, of listeners who wanted to dare their hand at this capricious delicacy, but Kitchenboy kept losing and finding the scrap of paper on which it was encrypted over dinner. So here he finally got it down for your challenge, cast in gold forever.

Soufflé (meaning puffed up, to breathe), that fragile princess of desserts, has a daunting reputation for its unpredictability, but taking a closer look at the mechanics of its creation may bring a more intimate perspective without robbing it of its romantic mystery.

Egg whites, on which soufflés ride, are made up of various albumen proteins, each playing a complex role in creating, stabilising & setting egg foams, till they coagulate as the bubble walls entrap the air bubbles. The air will expand on heating and the denatured (i.e. cooked) protein will hold up the whole shebang. Under-whipping results in large bubbles and over-whipping in clumping and collapse.

The perfect whisking point is just before it reaches strong peaks. Oil interferes with the stabilising of these foams, causing the bubble walls to drain back into the liquid (also why your bath foam disappears when adding oil or soap), as does salt & sugar. That's why even a tiny drop of oily yolk must be avoided. Plastic bowls, being polymers, readily retain oil traces and are therefore not advisable. Egg whites pick up copper ions from the bowl they are beaten in and this actually helps stabilise the foam and retard over-whipping. But once formed & stabilised, the foam can gently be folded into oily, sugary or salty mixtures.

This is the deservedly famous

Grand Marnier Soufflé recipe of chef Marc Geubert of *Ile de France.* who has on many occasions inspired me with his knowledge and forceful prowess of French cuisine. Watching him make a bouillabaisse on a furiously rolling boil is downright awesome. I know many envious chefs who dine there specifically for this soufflé, as I do. 'Yes, and they always try to figure out how I do it.' grumbled the eccentric *maestro.* We are duly grateful.

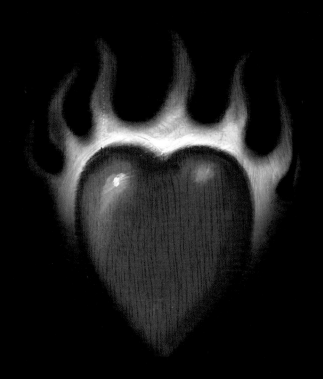

Kitchenboy loves you.

SOUFFLÉ

Marc Geubert's
GRAND MARNIER SOUFFLÉ
(Makes 6 servings)

12 egg yolks
300 g sugar
100 g flour
1 litre milk, scalded
6 tots Grand Marnier
12 egg whites
butter
sugar

• Combine the egg yolks and sugar with a whisk. • Only then incorporate the flour, mixing well. • Add the scalded (hot) milk and cook till it thickens, stirring continuously with a wooden spoon (he's adamant about this). Let this resultant custard cool completely, then add the liqueur. • Whisk the egg whites till firm and carefully fold the custard into it. • Butter 6 X 500 ml soufflé dishes and dust them with sugar. • Pour the mixture into the dishes. • Place them in a hot oven (300 °C) and let them rise (do not open the oven door). • Turn down the heat to 250 °C and cook for at least another 15 min. • Serve on the trot.
• Heat some more Grand Marnier in ladle and set aflame.
• Drool it into a gaatjie made in the top, where it will mingle with the soft centre.
Makes 6. Good luck.

Mushrooms 179-185:
Alternative fungi, various 183-5
Udon pot 181

Mussel & coconut milk soup 29

Noodles:
Asian, various 187-193
Toasted, mushroom broth & meat 117

Oysters 11

Pancakes:
Crêpes 233
Mandarin 109

Pasta, handmade 194-7
Peanut & chicken or guinea fowl soup, in 105
Perlemoen, steamed in shell 57
Perlemoen, blanching trick 56

Pork:
Belly, twice-cooked 141

Porridge, maize meal (see Mealiepap)

Potatoes:
Chips 204
Croquettes 205
Deep-fried, various 203-204
Mashed, saffron 201

Prawns, grilled 45

Rabbit:
Pan-fried 145
With raspberry-Campari sauce 145

Raspberry-Campari sauce 145

Rice:
Cooking perfect 209
Sushi 213

Salad:
Duck breast, cured 113
Dukkah 21
Girlfriend 33
Herb & bread 21
Tuna, seared, & rock sugar dressing 9

Sardines, grilled 92-3
Sashimi 12

Sauce:
Brandy & Coke marinade 137
Chakalaka 169
Chimichurri (vinegar-parsley) 129
Fresh chilli 165
Mushroom dashi, meat & noodles 117
Pineapple & guavadilla sauce 89
Raspberry-Campari sauce 145
Snoek & apricot jam basting 81

Shellfish 35-41:
Acid-cooked 85
Calamari, blanching trick 50-1
Calamari & chorizo, toss-fried 53
Cebisce, Peruvian 85
Curry, green 49
Mussel & coconut milk soup 29
Oysters 11
Perlemoen, steamed in shell 57
Perlemoen, blanching trick 56
Prawns, grilled 45
Steamed in cellophane parcel 61

Snoek & apricot jam 81

Soup:
Mussel & coconut milk 29
Udon pot 181

Steak tartare, Oriental 149
Smoked fish 71-3
Soufflé, Grand Marnier 237
Souskluitjies 229
Sushi rice 213
Tajine, Moroccan lamb 133
Tofu, various 215-7
Tuna, seared, & pepper-dhania crust 9
Udon pot 181
Vegetables, bright green 160-1
Vindaloo, duck 121
Vinegar-parsley sauce (chimichurri) 129

Dedicated to Robert Brozin